CONTENTS

INTRODUCTION

Welcome to *PE Core Activities Key Stages 1 and 2*. This resource has been written to support the delivery of the national curriculum. The core activities have been designed for pupils working between pre-curriculum/Early Key Stage 1 (age 4–5) and Key Stage 2 (age 10–11). 97 core activities have been written across 9 activity areas of the curriculum for physical education. Once a pupil has completed a core activity, they should progress to the next core activity in the sequence.

There is a separate resource available from 1st4sport.com entitled *PE Core Activities Key Stages 3 and 4*, which contains some overlap between Key Stages 2 and 3, and can be used along with this resource, depending on the ability of pupils.

The Core Activity Cards have been designed in such a way that pupils can complete each activity by following 3 instructions on a card, with minimal adult/leader help. With this in mind, a leader may choose to coordinate a number of varying ability groups to work on multiple core activities within a single lesson. Pupils may still need guidance selecting and setting up equipment, and they may benefit from having the core activity demonstrated.

'Leader sheets' accompany each Core Activity Card and feature possible lesson objectives and ways to differentiate and extend each activity. Of course, the suggestions on the leader sheet are by no means exhaustive or compulsory to use. The leader sheets are designed for use by a class teacher, a support staff member or a Key Stage 4/5 student to help pupils complete their core activities.

INTRODUCTION

What Will I Find on the CD?

The accompanying CD is split into 2 sections:

1 Introduction

2 Core Activity Cards.

Good luck!

PROGRESS TRACKER

	Pre-curriculum/ Early Key Stage 1 (Age 4–5)	Early Key Stage 1 (Age 5–6)	Middle to Upper Key Stage 1 (Age 6–7)	Upper Key Stage 1/Lower to Middle Key Stage 2 (Age 7–9)	Middle to Upper Key Stage 2 (Age 9–11)	Key Stage 2 to Key Stage 3 (Age 10–14)
Athletics		CORE ACTIVITY 1 CORE ACTIVITY 2 CORE ACTIVITY 3 CORE ACTIVITY 4 CORE ACTIVITY 5	CORE ACTIVITY 6 CORE ACTIVITY 7		CORE ACTIVITY 8 CORE ACTIVITY 9 CORE ACTIVITY 10	CORE ACTIVITY 11 CORE ACTIVITY 12 CORE ACTIVITY 13
Games	CORE ACTIVITY 1 CORE ACTIVITY 2 CORE ACTIVITY 3	CORE ACTIVITY 4 CORE ACTIVITY 5 CORE ACTIVITY 6 CORE ACTIVITY 7			CORE ACTIVITY 8 CORE ACTIVITY 9 CORE ACTIVITY 10	
Invasion Games			CORE ACTIVITY 1 CORE ACTIVITY 2	CORE ACTIVITY 6 CORE ACTIVITY 7 CORE ACTIVITY 3 CORE ACTIVITY 4 CORE ACTIVITY 5	CORE ACTIVITY 8 CORE ACTIVITY 9 CORE ACTIVITY 10	CORE ACTIVITY 11 CORE ACTIVITY 12 CORE ACTIVITY 13
Striking and Fielding			CORE ACTIVITY 1 CORE ACTIVITY 2 CORE ACTIVITY 3	CORE ACTIVITY 4 CORE ACTIVITY 5		CORE ACTIVITY 6 CORE ACTIVITY 7
Net/Wall Games			CORE ACTIVITY 1 CORE ACTIVITY 2 CORE ACTIVITY 3 CORE ACTIVITY 4 CORE ACTIVITY 5 CORE ACTIVITY 6	CORE ACTIVITY 7 CORE ACTIVITY 8 CORE ACTIVITY 9		CORE ACTIVITY 10 CORE ACTIVITY 11

PROGRESS TRACKER

	Pre-curriculum/ Early Key Stage 1 (Age 4–5)	Early Key Stage 1 (Age 5–6)	Middle to Upper Key Stage 1 (Age 6–7)	Upper Key Stage 1/Lower to Middle Key Stage 2 (Age 7–9)	Middle to Upper Key Stage 2 (Age 9–11)	Key Stage 2 to Key Stage 3 (Age 10–14)
Outdoor and Adventure		CORE ACTIVITY 1	CORE ACTIVITY 2		CORE ACTIVITY 6	CORE ACTIVITY 9
			CORE ACTIVITY 3		CORE ACTIVITY 7	CORE ACTIVITY 10
				CORE ACTIVITY 4	CORE ACTIVITY 8	
				CORE ACTIVITY 5		
Swimming	CORE ACTIVITY 1	CORE ACTIVITY 2	CORE ACTIVITY 3		CORE ACTIVITY 4	CORE ACTIVITY 7
					CORE ACTIVITY 5	CORE ACTIVITY 8
					CORE ACTIVITY 6	CORE ACTIVITY 9
Gymnastics	CORE ACTIVITY 1		CORE ACTIVITY 3	CORE ACTIVITY 7	CORE ACTIVITY 9	CORE ACTIVITY 13
	CORE ACTIVITY 2		CORE ACTIVITY 4	CORE ACTIVITY 8	CORE ACTIVITY 10	CORE ACTIVITY 14
			CORE ACTIVITY 5		CORE ACTIVITY 11	CORE ACTIVITY 15
			CORE ACTIVITY 6		CORE ACTIVITY 12	CORE ACTIVITY 16
Dance	CORE ACTIVITY 1		CORE ACTIVITY 2	CORE ACTIVITY 3	CORE ACTIVITY 5	CORE ACTIVITY 7
				CORE ACTIVITY 4	CORE ACTIVITY 6	CORE ACTIVITY 8

Note: These are guidelines only, and activities should be selected to match the ability of the pupils.

›››

ATHLETICS

MOVE BEANBAGS FROM HOOP TO HOOP

Activity 1, Early Key Stage 1 (Age 5–6)

1 Time how long it takes to move all beanbags

from hoop to hoop **1** at a time.

2 Test which is faster – running, walking,

hopping or skipping?

>>> LEADER NOTES

Objectives

Pupils should:

- be able to evaluate their performance using time
- know and understand quicker and slower ways of travelling
- develop fundamental movement skills
- engage in competitive (both against self and others) and cooperative physical activities in a range of increasingly challenging situations.

Differentiation and Extension

Easier

- Place the hoops closer.
- Use fewer beanbags.
- Work in relay teams.

Harder

- Place the hoops further apart.
- Introduce a time limit.
- Use more beanbags.

Extension

- Carry or dribble other balls or equipment.
- Vary the ways of travel.

Full Activity Description

Using different ways of travelling (eg running, walking, hopping and skipping) and following different pathways or courses, see how fast or far you can go in challenges such as:

- How fast can you move 5 beanbags from 1 hoop to another?
- How many red cones can you touch in 30 seconds, 20 seconds, 10 seconds etc?

HOW MANY CONES CAN YOU TOUCH IN THE TIME?

Activity 2, Early Key Stage 1 (Age 5–6)

Count the cones you can touch in:

1 **30** seconds

2 **20** seconds

3 **10** seconds.

»» LEADER NOTES

Objectives

Pupils should:

- be able to evaluate their performance using time
- know and understand quicker and slower ways of travelling
- develop fundamental movement skills
- engage in competitive (both against self and others) and cooperative physical activities in a range of increasingly challenging situations.

Differentiation and Extension

Easier

- Place the cones closer together.
- Use fewer cones.
- Work in relay teams.

Harder

- Place the cones further apart.
- Introduce a time limit.
- Use more cones.

Extension

- Carry or dribble other balls or equipment.
- Vary the ways of travel.

Full Activity Description

Using different ways of travelling (eg running, walking, hopping and skipping) and following different pathways or courses, see how fast or far you can go in challenges such as:

- How fast can you move 5 beanbags from 1 hoop to another?
- How many red cones can you touch in 30 seconds, 20 seconds, 10 seconds etc?

HOW FAR AND HIGH CAN YOU THROW?

Activity 3, Middle to Upper Key Stage 1 (Age 6–7)

1 Run further than your throw in **3** seconds.

2 Throw higher than it takes to do **5** jumps.

3 Beat your **scores** by:

throwing underarm, throwing overarm, rolling and sliding.

»» LEADER NOTES

Objectives

Pupils should:

- be able to attempt a variety of throwing techniques in order to improve accuracy
- know and understand how the position of the body affects throwing performance
- develop fundamental movement skills, become increasingly competent and confident, and access a broad range of activities to extend their agility, balance and coordination
- engage in competitive (both against self and others) and cooperative physical activities in a range of increasingly challenging situations.

Differentiation and Extension

Easier

- Use smaller, heavier balls.
- Give a running and jumping head start.
- Use a partner to throw while the pupil performs the activities.

Harder

- Use less aerodynamic equipment.
- Increase the running distance and number of jumps to perform.
- Throw from kneeling, sitting and lying positions.

Extension

- Hit the balls.
- Aim for targets as opposed to completing activities.

Full Activity Description

Using different ways of throwing (eg underarm, overarm, pushing, rolling and sliding) and different types of equipment, see how far, high or accurately you can throw in challenges such as:

- Can you throw further than you can run in 3 seconds or jump in 5 jumps?
- Can you throw nearer the middle of the hoop?
- Can you bounce the ball higher than the mark on the wall?
- How high up the wall can you bounce the ball?

HOW ACCURATELY CAN YOU THROW?

Activity 4, Middle to Upper Key Stage 1 (Age 6–7)

1 Throw to the middle of the target.

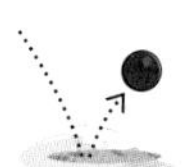

2 Bounce a ball high up the wall.

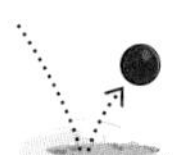

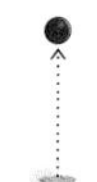

3 Bounce a ball to hit a mark high up the wall.

LEADER NOTES

Objectives

Pupils should:

- be able to attempt a variety of throwing techniques in order to improve accuracy
- know and understand how the position of the body affects throwing performance
- develop fundamental movement skills, become increasingly competent and confident, and access a broad range of activities to extend their agility, balance and coordination
- engage in competitive (both against self and others) and cooperative physical activities in a range of increasingly challenging situations.

Differentiation and Extension

Easier

- Use smaller, heavier balls.
- Move the targets closer and lower.
- Award points for the ball landing close to the target.

Harder

- Use less aerodynamic equipment.
- Increase the target distances and heights.
- Throw from kneeling, sitting and lying positions.

Extension

- Hit the balls.
- Aim for moving targets.

Full Activity Description

Using different ways of throwing (eg underarm, overarm, pushing, rolling and sliding) and different types of equipment, see how far, high or accurately you can throw in challenges such as:

- Can you throw further than you can run in 3 seconds or jump in 5 jumps?
- Can you throw nearer the middle of the hoop?
- Can you bounce the ball higher than the mark on the wall?
- How high up the wall can you bounce the ball?

JUMP IN DIFFERENT WAYS

Activity 5, Middle to Upper Key Stage 1 (Age 6–7)

1 Jump across an area in less than **5** jumps.

2 Jump **longer** than your body length.

3 Beat your **scores** by trying the **different** jumps.

LEADER NOTES

Objectives

Pupils should:

- be able to perform 1:2, 2:2, 2:1 and 1:1 jumps
- know and understand how different jumping techniques affect distance travelled
- develop fundamental movement skills, become increasingly competent and confident, and access a broad range of activities to extend their agility, balance and coordination
- engage in competitive (both against self and others) and cooperative physical activities in a range of increasingly challenging situations.

Differentiation and Extension

Easier

- Add smaller targets to jump to before the overall target.
- Record a best attempt and award points each time it is beaten.
- Jump with a partner of similar ability.

Harder

- Increase the distance of the area and choose a taller person's height to jump.
- Develop a 'league' with promotion once a set and height are achieved.
- Do not allow a run-up before a jump.

Extension

- Explore ways of measuring jumps (eg steps and handspans).

Full Activity Description

Using different ways of jumping (eg 2 feet to 2 feet, 2 feet to 1 foot, 1 foot to same foot, 1 foot to opposite foot), see how far, high or long you can jump in challenges such as:

- Can you skip without stopping for 10 seconds, 20 seconds etc?
- Can you jump across a space (eg a badminton court) in less than 5 jumps?
- Can you jump further than the distance between your head and feet when you are lying down?

TRY DIFFERENT WAYS OF RUNNING, JUMPING AND THROWING

Activity 6, Upper Key Stage 1/Lower to Middle Key Stage 2 (Age 7–9)

1 Try running:

- short steps, long strides
- straight arms, bent arms, swinging arms.

2 Try jumping:

- from 1 foot
- from 2 feet.

3 Try throwing:

- underarm
- overarm
- pushing
- pulling
- slinging.

LEADER NOTES

Objectives

Pupils should:

- be able to run, jump and throw using a variety of techniques
- know and understand how altering the movement of any parts of the body during performance affects end results
- become increasingly competent and confident, and access a broad range of opportunities to extend their agility, balance and coordination
- learn how to use skills in different ways and link them to make actions
- develop an understanding of how to improve in different physical activities.

Differentiation and Extension

Easier

- Mirror and match movements from a partner.
- Add small, attainable targets.

Harder

- Increase the performance distances.
- Introduce competition between pupils and award points for distances covered.

Extension

- Explore different ways of throwing equipment and measuring distances covered (eg by feet or body lengths).

Full Activity Description

In small groups, investigate and compare the effectiveness of different styles of:

- running (eg short steps, long strides, straight arms, bent arms, swinging arms)
- jumping (eg off 1 foot, off 2 feet)
- throwing (eg underarm, overarm, pushing, pulling, slinging).

Decide which styles you like best and see if you can go faster, higher or further.

RUN IN A RELAY TEAM

Activity 7, Upper Key Stage 1/Lower to Middle Key Stage 2 (Age 7–9)

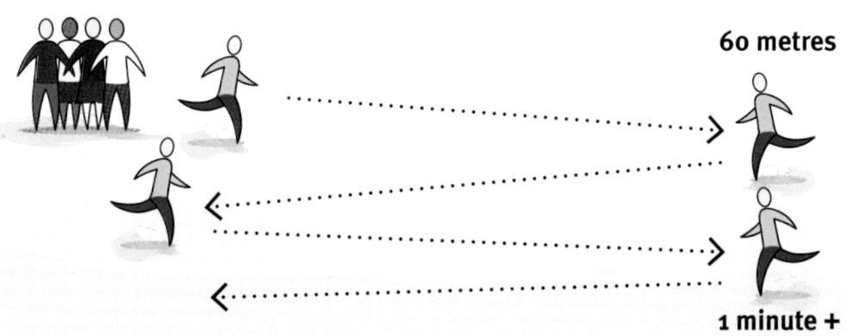

1 As a team, run as fast as you can for **60** metres.

2 Run as far as you can in **1** minute.

3 Run for as **long** as possible. Write your distance down.

»» LEADER NOTES

Objectives

Pupils should:

- be able to run as part of a relay team
- know and understand the difference between a 'sprint' and a 'distance' race
- become increasingly competent and confident, and access a broad range of opportunities to extend their agility, balance and coordination
- learn how to use skills in different ways and link them to make actions
- develop an understanding of how to improve in different physical activities.

Differentiation and Extension

Easier

- Give a less able team a 3, 2, 1 countdown to start their run.
- Give points for completion of a race.
- Let the next runner take a 'run-up' to tag the oncoming runner.

Harder

- Increase the performance distances.
- Introduce competition between pupils and award points for the quickest times.
- Mix abilities within the team.

Extension

- Run on circular athletic tracks.
- Run on rough/cross-country terrain and/or add obstacles.
- Explore alternatives to running.

Full Activity Description

In teams of 4, find out ways of running the:

- fastest time as a relay team over a shared distance of 60m
- longest distance as a relay team over times of, for example, 1 minute, 1 minute 30 seconds, 2 minutes, 3 minutes.

HOW FAR CAN YOU RUN IN A TIME?

Activity 8, Middle to Upper Key Stage 2 (Age 9–11)

1 **Measure** how far you can run in the **set** times.

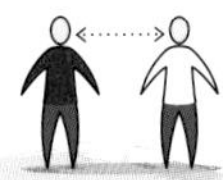

2 Try to run faster, over a **longer** distance.

3 **Set** yourself a target for your next run.

LEADER NOTES

Objectives

Pupils should:

- be able to set a realistic individual performance target
- know and understand the further the run, the more the runners need to pace themselves
- develop an understanding of how to improve in different physical activities and sports, and learn how to evaluate and recognise their own success.

Differentiation and Extension

Easier

- Run for a shorter time/practise improving shorter-distance times only.
- Give points for completion of a race.
- Run the race as a 2-person 'tag team'.

Harder

- Incorporate other skills, such as skipping, jumping and hopping.
- Introduce competition between pupils and award points for the quickest times.
- Incorporate changes of direction and/or obstacles into the courses.

Extension

- Explore completing races with equipment (eg dribbling a ball).
- Explore completing outside in a wooded area.

Full Activity Description

Measure how far you can run in:

- 5 seconds
- 30 seconds
- 2 minutes.

See if you can run faster so you can improve the distance you go, and set your own targets for improvement.

››› HOW HIGH AND FAR CAN YOU JUMP?

Activity 9, Middle to Upper Key Stage 2 (Age 9–11)

1 **Measure** how high and far you can jump by:

– standing and jumping

– running up and jumping

– jumping after a step and a hop.

  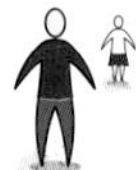

2 Try to jump higher and further.

3 **Set** yourself a target for your next jump.

LEADER NOTES

Objectives

Pupils should:

- be able to identify which method of jumping is the most effective
- know and understand the importance of landing with bent knees
- develop an understanding of how to improve in different physical activities and sports, and learn how to evaluate and recognise their own success.

Differentiation and Extension

Easier

- Jump over imaginary heights and distance markers.
- Allow 'no jumps'.
- Allow 3 or more chances to gain their best score.

Harder

- Jump over physical heights (eg bamboo canes) and past visible markers (eg cones 0.5m apart).
- Define and use 'no jump' rules.
- Only allow a 2-footed landing falling forwards.

Extension

- Explore combining a sequence of jumps.

Full Activity Description

Measure how long or high you can jump using:

- standing jumps
- jumps with run-ups
- combination jumps (eg 2-footed jump, step, hop).

See if you can improve on the distance or height you jump, and set your own targets for improvement.

>>> HOW HIGH AND FAR CAN YOU THROW?

Activity 10, Middle to Upper Key Stage 2 (Age 9–11)

1 **Measure** how high and far you can throw by:

– bouncing a ball **over** a barrier

– running up and throwing

– throwing different equipment.

2 Try to throw higher and further.

3 **Set** yourself a target for your next throw.

LEADER NOTES

Objectives

Pupils should:

- be able to identify which method of throwing is the most effective
- know and understand the importance of throwing and following through
- develop an understanding of how to improve in different physical activities and sports, and learn how to evaluate and recognise their own success.

Differentiation and Extension

Easier

- Throw over imaginary heights and distance markers.
- Allow pupils 3 or more chances to gain their best score.
- Allow underarm throws and rolling the ball.

Harder

- Throw over physical heights (eg basketball hoops) and past visible markers (eg cones 2m apart).
- Only allow balls that land in an identified area.
- Use larger and lighter balls.

Extension

- Explore sending the ball in other ways (eg hitting the ball).

Full Activity Description

Measure how well you can throw:

- for height (eg bounce the ball and try to clear the barrier)
- for distance
- with run-ups and without
- using different equipment (eg hoops, large and small balls, quoits mini-discus, beanbags).

See if you can improve the distance or height you throw, and set your own targets for improvement.

HOW QUICKLY AND HOW FAR CAN YOU ACCELERATE FOR?

Activity 11, Key Stage 2/Key Stage 3 (Age 10–14)

8 seconds
12 seconds

50 metres
100 metres

1 In your group, take turns to run the **set** time or distance.

2 Use cones to mark how far each runner has travelled

after **1, 2, 3, 4** and **5** seconds.

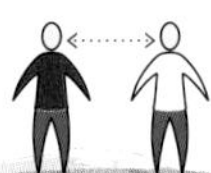 

3 Try to **improve** the distance between the cones by

practising starting and accelerating techniques.

LEADER NOTES

Objectives

Pupils should:

- be able to improve on their initial race times through the use of starting and accelerating techniques
- know and understand skill elements of starting and accelerating in sprint races
- develop a broader range of skills
- enjoy communicating, collaborating and competing with each other
- develop an understanding of how to improve and learn how to evaluate and recognise their own success
- become more competent, confident and expert in their techniques
- understand what makes a performance effective and how to apply these principles to their own and others' work.

Differentiation and Extension

Easier

- Decrease distance and time targets.
- Encourage pupils to set individual targets.
- Focus on either starting or accelerating techniques.

Harder

- Place cones at the finish as well as the start.
- Place runners next to each other to encourage competition.
- Repeat over longer times and distances (with cones placed at comparably increased distances).

Extension

- Focus on keeping an even pace as opposed to accelerating.
- Race in a form other than running.

Full Activity Description

The purpose of this activity is for pupils to find out how long they can keep accelerating and how long they can sustain maximum pace. Working in small groups, use cones to mark how far each runner reaches after 1, 2, 3, 4 and 5 seconds when running for 8–12 seconds or for a distance of 50–100m. Compare the distance between each cone and see how it relates to the distance covered in the rest of the time.

Develop starting and accelerating technique to improve speed over this distance and longer sprints. Repeat over longer time spans in longer runs (eg the distance covered in a 40–60-second run after 10, 20 and 30 seconds and the distance covered after 30, 60, 90, 120 and 180 seconds in runs of more than 3 minutes).

FIND THE BEST RUN-UP DISTANCE FOR YOUR LONG JUMP

Activity 12, Key Stage 2/Key Stage 3 (Age 10–14)

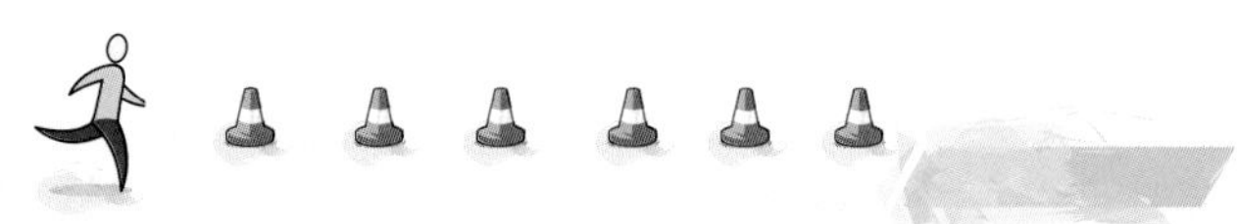

1 Use cones to measure **1, 3, 7, 11, 15** and **19** paces

from your jump board.

2 Perform jumps from each of your **measured** distances

to find which run-up distance gives you the best jump.

3 Measure your jump from where your **toe** touches the jump board

to the first **mark** made on the sand/floor.

LEADER NOTES

Objectives

Pupils should:

- be able to consistently perform a legal long jump from their optimum run-up distance
- know and understand where legal long jumps are measured from and to
- develop a broader range of skills
- enjoy communicating, collaborating and competing with each other
- develop an understanding of how to improve and learn how to evaluate and recognise their own success
- become more competent, confident and expert in their techniques
- understand what makes a performance effective and how to apply these principles to their own and others' work.

Differentiation and Extension

Easier

- Measure from the take-off toe instead of the board.
- Use a collapsible triangle/aid in the pit to encourage high and long jumps.
- Use visible targets in the pit for pupils to aim at.

Harder

- Use an umpire to call no jumps.
- Attempt the jump leading from and jumping from the non-dominant foot.
- Incorporate combination and triple jumps.

Extension

- Explore arm actions throughout jump manoeuvres (eg stretching upwards with both arms).

Full Activity Description

The purpose of this activity is to investigate the effect of the length of a run-up on the distance achieved in a jump. Pupils should measure the distance they jump off the following run-ups: 1 pace; 3 paces; 7 paces; 11 paces; 15 paces; 19 paces. For the purpose of the investigation, jumps should be measured from the toe of the jumping foot to the nearest mark made in the pit.

When they have discovered the optimum distance for their own run-up, pupils should work out how to make that run consistent so they jump obeying the rules of competition.

CHANGE YOUR BODY POSITION TO HELP IMPROVE YOUR THROWING ACCURACY

Activity 13, Key Stage 2/Key Stage 3 (Age 10–14)

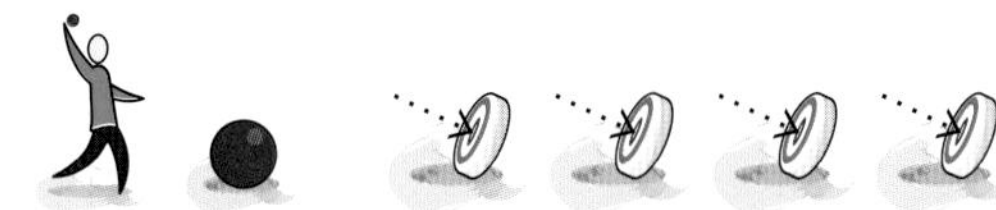

1 Standing behind your line, throw a ball at each of the targets in turn.

2 Change the **position** of your **shoulders**

for every throw (right shoulders forward, then left shoulders forward).

3 Change the **position** of your **feet** for every throw.

4 Find out which body **positions** produced

your most accurate throws.

LEADER NOTES

Objectives

Pupils should:

- be able to consciously change their body positions before completing a throwing action
- know and understand how changing the body position during throwing affects performance
- develop a broader range of skills
- enjoy communicating, collaborating and competing with each other
- develop an understanding of how to improve and learn how to evaluate and recognise their own success
- become more competent, confident and expert in their techniques
- understand what makes a performance effective and how to apply these principles to their own and others' work.

Differentiation and Extension

Easier

- Use a leader to physically hold the thrower's body steady in the adopted position.
- Count throws that land within a target's surrounding areas.
- Use lightly weighted, easy to hold and dynamic throwing objects (eg tennis balls).

Harder

- Only count throws that hit or land on a target.
- Only allow progression to the next target once the previous throw is successful in hitting the target.
- Use sitting and kneeling in addition to standing throws.

Extension

- Use a variety of equipment, including non-aerodynamic flying objects.

Full Activity Description

The purpose of this activity is to investigate the relationship between the height or trajectory of a throw and the distance achieved. Using pushing, pulling and slinging actions, and a variety of equipment, pupils try to hit targets or markers at varying distances from the point of throw (eg using pulling action and a tennis ball or a javelin, with markers at 3m, 5m, 7m, 11m, 15m and 20m). Pupils find out how the positions of the body and feet change as the target gets further away. Set a target near the maximum distance and have pupils try to reach it or go further.

››› GAMES

THROW THE BEANBAG INTO THE HOOP

Activity 1, Pre-curriculum/Lower Key Stage 1 (Age 4–5)

1 Do not cross the line.

2 Person **A**: Throw the beanbag **into** the hoop.

3 Person **B**: Stop the beanbag going into the hoop.

LEADER NOTES

Objectives

Pupils should:

- be able to throw objects towards a target
- know and understand the term 'defend' and the role of a defender
- develop fundamental movement skills, becoming increasingly competent and confident
- engage in competitive and cooperative physical activities in a range of increasingly challenging situations.

Differentiation and Extension

Easier

- Increase number of beanbags per person.
- Use larger hoops.
- Move hoops closer to line.

Harder

- Throw beanbags at the same time.
- Change hoop targets to cones/markers.

Extension

- Remove opponent and work on accuracy.
- Play 2 v 2 and small teams.

Full Activity Description

The aim of the game is to throw beanbags into your opponent's hoop to score points. The game is played 1 v 1.

Set up a 'court', with a line dividing 2 players. Position a hoop on either side of the line, 1–2m from the line. Each player tries to throw 3 beanbags into the hoop on the opposite side of the line, while their opponent tries to stop them without actually touching the hoop. After 1 player has thrown 3 beanbags, the other player has a go. Once the children have learnt how to defend their hoop well, add a second hoop about a child's stride away from the first.

ROLL THE BALL OVER THE LINE

Activity 2, Pre-curriculum/Lower Key Stage 1 (Age 4–5)

1 Do not cross the line.

2 Person **A:** Roll the ball **over** the line.

3 Person **B:** Stop the ball going over the line.

LEADER NOTES

Objectives

Pupils should:

- be able to move to defend an oncoming target
- know and understand how to defend a large area
- develop fundamental movement skills, becoming increasingly competent and confident
- engage in competitive and cooperative physical activities in a range of increasingly challenging situations.

Differentiation and Extension

Easier

- Use large balls.
- Move the lines closer together.

Harder

- Move the lines further apart.
- Change shape and size of equipment.

Extension

- Increase number of players on each side.
- Use hockey sticks and balls.
- Kick balls.

Full Activity Description

The aim of the game is to score points by sliding a beanbag or rolling a ball over your opponent's line. The game is played 1 v 1 or 2 v 2.

Set up 2 parallel lines, 3–5m apart (make sure there are sides to the court). The children should position themselves on either side of the lines, but may put their hands into the space between. The opponents try to intercept the ball or beanbag and then try to score themselves.

THROW THE BEANBAG, JUMP INTO AND OUT OF THE HOOP

Activity 3, Pre-curriculum/Lower Key Stage 1 (Age 4–5)

1 Person **A:** Throw the beanbag.

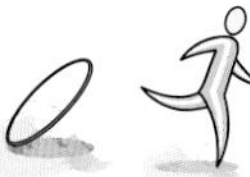

2 Person **B:** Return the beanbag to the hoop quickly.

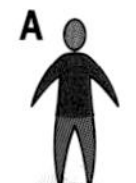

3 Person **A:** Jump into and out of the hoop

before the beanbag is put into the hoop.

LEADER NOTES

Objectives

Pupils should:

- be able to throw a beanbag forwards in an overarm motion
- know and understand the term 'fielder' and the role of a fielder
- develop fundamental movement skills, becoming increasingly competent and confident
- engage in competitive and cooperative physical activities in a range of increasingly challenging situations.

Differentiation and Extension

Easier

- Have fewer fielders.
- Extend throwing distance area.
- Pass the beanbag between all fielders before returning it to the hoop.
- 'Batter' bounces a ball to increase distance travelling.

Harder

- 'Batter' throws with non-dominant arm.
- Decrease throwing distance area.
- Fielders move and pass between themselves to return the beanbag to the hoop faster.

Extension

- Hit the beanbags with a bat/racket (with[out] hitting tee).
- Kick the beanbags.
- Use balls and playing areas of varying sizes and shapes.
- Change the location of the hoop/number of hoops.

Full Activity Description

The aim of the game is for the thrower (batter) to score as many points as possible by throwing beanbags into a channel and then counting how many times they can move in and out of a hoop before fielders retrieve the beanbags. The game is played 1 v 1, 1 v 2 or 1 v 3.

1 player stands in a hoop and throws beanbags down a marked channel. The other players stand behind the thrower and run to retrieve the beanbags after they have been thrown. There should be 1 beanbag for each fielder to retrieve. Players take it in turns to throw. Once the children know how to play the game successfully, the fielders should stand in the throwing channel to try to intercept the beanbags.

TOUCH THE CONE WITH THE BALL

Activity 4, Middle to Upper Key Stage 1 (Age 6–7)

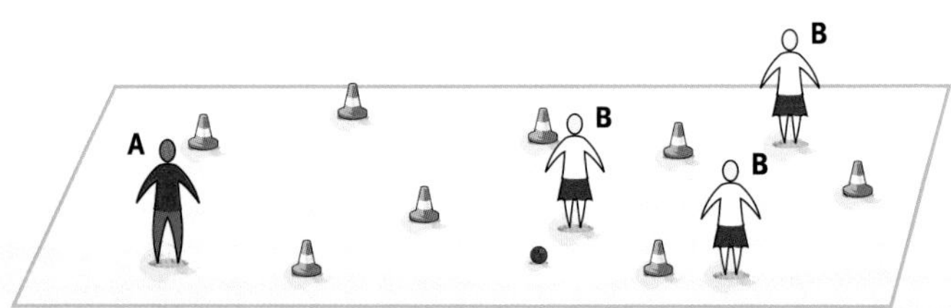

1 Person **B:** Throw and catch the ball without moving.

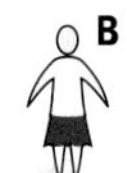

2 Person **B:** Touch the cones with the ball.

Do not touch the **same** cone **twice** in a row.

3 Person **A:** Try to touch the ball.

LEADER NOTES

Objectives

Pupils should:

- be able to throw and catch a ball with a team member
- know and understand the term 'intercept'
- continue to develop fundamental movement skills, becoming increasingly competent and confident
- access a broad range of opportunities to extend their agility, balance and coordination, individually and with others
- engage in competitive and cooperative physical activities in a range of increasingly challenging situations.

Differentiation and Extension

Easier

- Play in a larger area.
- Use a larger ball.

Harder

- Nominate specific cones or colours for points.
- Knock over the cones to gain points.
- Use smaller equipment/different shapes.

Extension

- Use rolling and stopping/kicking or pushing instead of throwing and catching.
- Use bats/sticks.

Full Activity Description

The aim is to score as many points as possible before the defender touches the ball.

Lay out 4–8 cones in a playing area that is between $5m^2$ and $10m^2$ in size. Play with a team of 3 attackers against 1 defender. The 3 attackers must use throwing and catching skills, and cannot move with the ball. Their aim is to score points by touching the cones with the ball as many times as they can. They can touch the cones in any order, but must not touch the same cone twice in a row.

CATCH THE BALL BEFORE IT BOUNCES

Activity 5, Middle to Upper Key Stage 1 (Age 6–7)

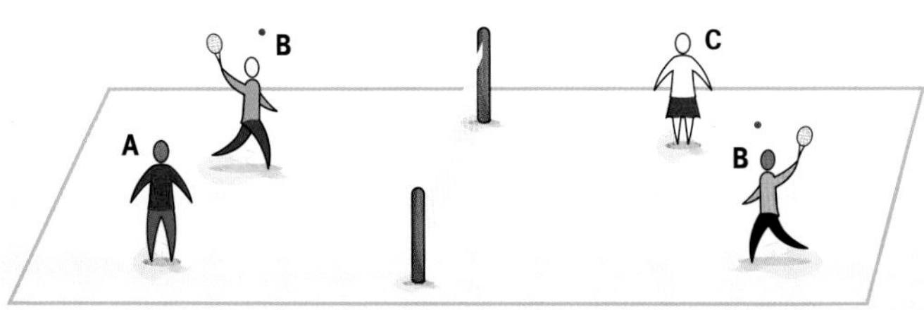

1 Person **A:** 'Feed' the ball to Person **B.**

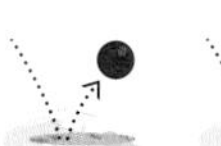

2 Person **B:** Throw or hit the ball so it bounces twice.

3 Person **C:** Try to catch the bouncing ball.

>>> LEADER NOTES

Objectives

Pupils should:

- be able to catch a moving ball
- know and understand the term 'feed'
- continue to develop fundamental movement skills, becoming increasingly competent and confident
- access a broad range of opportunities to extend their agility, balance and coordination, individually and with others
- engage in competitive and cooperative physical activities in a range of increasingly challenging situations.

Differentiation and Extension

Easier

- Bounce the ball on your own side of the net first.
- Take turns at catching and throwing.

Harder

- Play continuous rallies.
- Play against a wall.

Extension

- Throw and catch beanbags on a bat.
- Play games restricting player movement.

Full Activity Description

The aim is to score points by throwing or hitting a ball over a net so it bounces twice, with the first bounce in the court area.

Play the game on a marked court with about 2–3m^2 on each side of a low net. Play the game 2 v 2 – each pair should have 1 player with a racket and 1 without. The player who does not have a racket 'feeds' a ball to their partner, who then tries to hit it over the net into their opponents' court. When the ball goes over the net, the player without the racket on the other side tries to intercept or catch the ball before it bounces twice, before feeding it to their own partner. When their hitting skills improve, players can catch the ball themselves before hitting it back, and go on to a continuous rally.

CATCH THE BALL BEFORE IT BOUNCES

Activity 6, Middle to Upper Key Stage 1 (Age 6–7)

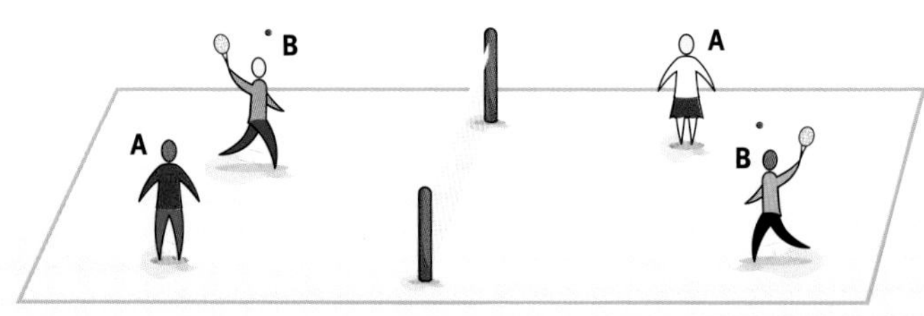

1 Person **A:** 'Feed' the ball to Person **B.**

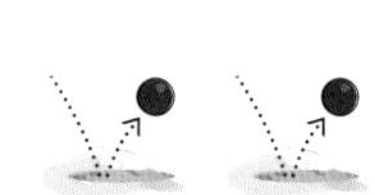

2 Throw or hit the ball so it bounces twice.

3 Catch the ball and **return** it over the net quickly.

LEADER NOTES

Objectives

Pupils should:

- be able to catch a moving ball
- know and understand the term 'feed'
- continue to develop fundamental movement skills, becoming increasingly competent and confident
- access a broad range of opportunities to extend their agility, balance and coordination, individually and with others
- engage in competitive and cooperative physical activities in a range of increasingly challenging situations.

Differentiation and Extension

Easier

- Bounce the ball on your own side of the net first.
- Take turns at catching and throwing.

Harder

- Play continuous rallies.
- Play against a wall.

Extension

- Throw and catch beanbags on a bat.
- Play games restricting player movement.

Full Activity Description

The aim is to score points by throwing or hitting a ball over a net so it bounces twice, with the first bounce in the court area.

Play the game on a marked court with about 2–3m² on each side of a low net. Play the game 2 v 2 – each pair should have 1 player with a racket and 1 without. The player who does not have a racket 'feeds' a ball to their partner, who then tries to hit it over the net into their opponents' court. When the ball goes over the net, the player without the racket on the other side tries to intercept or catch the ball before it bounces twice, before feeding it to their own partner. When their hitting skills improve, players can catch the ball themselves before hitting it back, and go on to a continuous rally.

HIT THE BALL AND RUN WITH THE BEANBAG

Activity 7, Middle to Upper Key Stage 1 (Age 6–7)

1 Person **A:** 'Feed' the ball to the batter.

2 Batter: **Hit** the ball. Run around each of the cones

and drop the beanbag on the furthest cone.

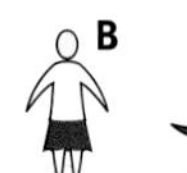

3 Person **B:** Run to **return** the ball to base.

LEADER NOTES

Objectives

Pupils should:

- be able to hit a moving ball with a bat
- know and understand the term 'bat' and the role of a 'batter'
- continue to develop fundamental movement skills, becoming increasingly competent and confident
- access a broad range of opportunities to extend their agility, balance and coordination, individually and with others
- engage in competitive and cooperative physical activities in a range of increasingly challenging situations.

Differentiation and Extension

Easier

- Use larger balls.
- Place bases closer together and nearer batter.

Harder

- Place bases further apart.
- Use a variation of 'feeding' techniques (eg kicking).

Extension

- Throw the ball instead of hitting.
- Test, evaluate and discuss the types of balls that are better for batters or fielders.

Full Activity Description

The aim is for the batter to hit a ball into a field and then run as far as possible around a circuit of bases before the fielding team returns the ball to the fielding base.

Play the game with 1 batter, 1 feeder and 3 fielders. The feeder throws the ball to the batter, who then hits it into an arc with an angle of 60–90°. The batter scores by carrying a beanbag to 1 of 4 bases placed in a semicircle, running around these in an anticlockwise direction. The first base is worth 1 point, the second 2 points and so on. The batter can only run until the fielding team returns the ball to the fielding base. The batter has 4 consecutive goes and adds up the points from each hit. Everyone takes turns to bat, field and feed.

››› GET THE BALL TO THE OPPOSITE GOAL

Activity 8, Upper Key Stage 2/Key Stage 3 (Age 10–14)

1 Red players stay in the **middle** section and stop

the blue players from scoring/keeping the ball.

2 Red players score in the **smaller** goals.

3 Blue players score in the **large** goal.

LEADER NOTES

Objectives

Pupils should:

- be able to think about and plan their next move before moving
- know and understand the term 'space' and how to utilise space within a game
- continue to implement and develop a broader range of skills, learning how to use them in different ways
- enjoy communicating, collaborating and competing with each other
- develop an understanding of how to succeed in different activities and sports, and learn how to evaluate and recognise their own success
- become more competent, confident and expert in their techniques
- develop the confidence and interest to get involved in exercise, sports and activities outside school.

Differentiation and Extension

Easier

- Play with even-sided teams.
- Play with '3 chances' to cross over a boundary within a game.

Harder

- Only allow scoring when in a 'scoring game'.
- Only allow limited numbers within a 'scoring game'.

Extension

- Play the game with different equipment (eg hockey, football, rugby, netball).
- Play on wide or narrow short pitches.
- Play with even-sided teams, with the team in possession having no boundaries, and the non-possession team having to remain in the middle.

Full Activity Description

The aim of the game is to set up an attack, and shoot or score without the defenders touching the ball.

Play the game 4 v 3 or 5 v 4, on a pitch that is divided into 3 sections. The larger team (mainly attackers) starts with the ball in 1 end section and tries to score a goal in the other end section. The smaller team (mainly defenders) is only allowed in the middle section of the pitch and has to try to stop the opposition from scoring or keeping possession. The smaller team scores when it gets the ball in 1 of 2 goals in the larger team's starting section.

››› HIT THE BALL AND MAKE IT BOUNCE TWICE

Activity 9, Upper Key Stage 2/Key Stage 3 (Age 10–14)

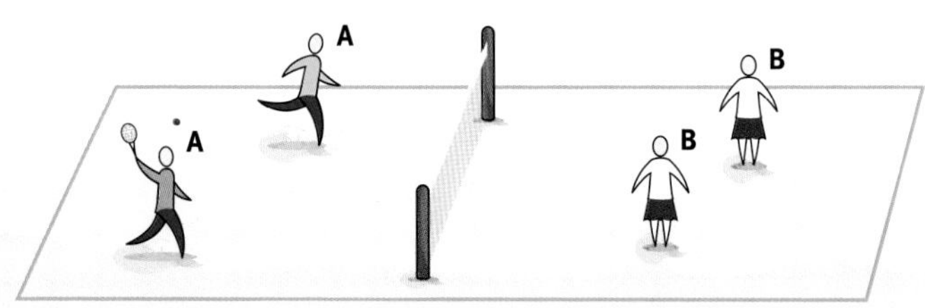

1 Hit the ball, trying to make it bounce twice

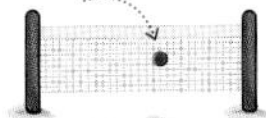

on the opposite side of the net.

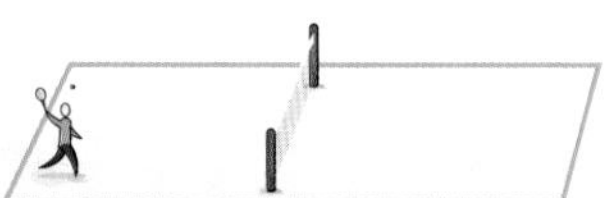

2 Serve from the **back** of the court.

3 Take turns to hit the ball. Play in teams of **2–3**.

LEADER NOTES

Objectives

Pupils should:

- be able to throw and catch continuously over a net
- know and understand the term 'volley' and be able to identify a volley within a game
- continue to implement and develop a broader range of skills, learning how to use them in different ways
- enjoy communicating, collaborating and competing with each other
- develop an understanding of how to succeed in different activities and sports, and learn how to evaluate and recognise their own success
- become more competent, confident and expert in their techniques
- develop the confidence and interest to get involved in exercise, sports and activities outside school.

Differentiation and Extension

Easier

- Use a larger ball.
- Let the ball bounce twice before hitting it.

Harder

- Play on a larger court.
- Use a higher net.
- Play to opposite diagonal corners.

Extension

- Play with tennis equipment.
- Use volleyball-type skills in teams of 3–4.

Full Activity Description

The aim of the game is to score points by making the ball bounce twice on the opponents' side of the net. The first bounce must land in the court.

Play in teams of 2 or 3 on a court that is short and wide. Serve from the back of the court. Players on the same team should take it in turns to hit the ball.

»» HIT THE BALL INTO THE SCORING AREAS

Activity 10, Upper Key Stage 2/Key Stage 3 (Age 10–14)

1 Red players take it in turns to bowl to the blue players.

2 The batter **hits** the ball but **only** runs if the ball lands

in a scoring area.

3 The red team bowls **20** balls before changing teams.

LEADER NOTES

Objectives

Pupils should:

- be able to hit a ball in a predetermined direction
- know and understand how to aim and hit in a predetermined direction
- continue to implement and develop a broader range of skills, learning how to use them in different ways
- enjoy communicating, collaborating and competing with each other
- develop an understanding of how to succeed in different activities and sports, and learn how to evaluate and recognise their own success
- become more competent, confident and expert in their techniques
- develop the confidence and interest to get involved in exercise, sports and activities outside school.

Differentiation and Extension

Easier

- Use a racket with a larger surface area (eg a tennis racket).
- Let the batter choose whether they wish to run or stay.

Harder

- Further define scoring areas into high scoring parts.
- Define rules to make a batter 'out'.
- Attempt to reach a set number of 'runs' each innings.

Extension

- Attempt to reach a set number of runs each innings.
- Adapt area of cricket dimensions.

Full Activity Description

The aim of the game is to score points or runs by running around bases or between wickets.

Play the game with 2 batters against 4–6 fielders, who take it in turns to bowl. Players may only run when they hit the ball into marked areas of the field. Pairs of batters play an innings of 20–30 balls.

INVASION GAMES

»» BOUNCE THE BALL AND KNOCK OVER THE SKITTLE

Activity 1, Upper Key Stage 1/Lower to Middle Key Stage 2 (Age 7–9)

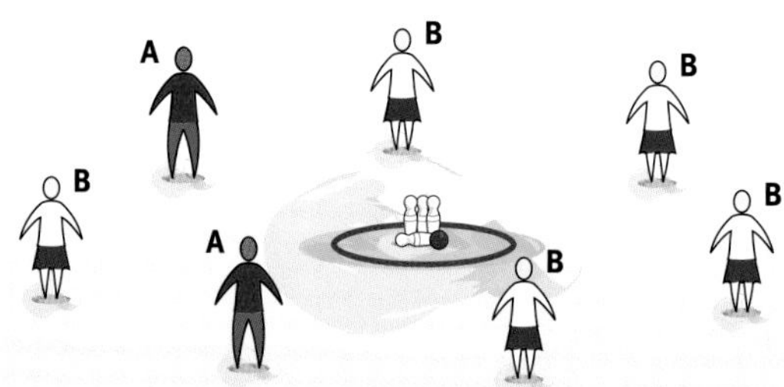

1 Do not enter the circle.

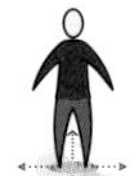
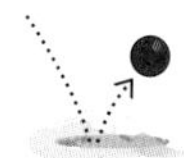

Only move when bouncing the ball.

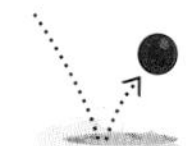

2 Bounce the ball and knock over the skittle.

3 Person **B:** Take a free pass after scoring

(outside of the circle).

LEADER NOTES

Objectives

Pupils should:

- be able to bounce a ball in the direction of a target
- know and understand the terms 'bouncing' and 'travelling'
- continue to develop fundamental movement skills and become increasingly competent and confident
- apply and develop a broader range of skills, learning how to use them in different ways
- be able to engage in competitive and cooperative physical activities in a range of increasingly challenging situations, and enjoy communicating, collaborating and competing with each other
- start to develop an understanding of how to improve, and learn how to evaluate and recognise their own success.

Differentiation and Extension

Easier

- Allow no movement with the ball.
- Roll the ball.

Harder

- Change more able pupils to the smaller team.
- Play 3 v 3.

Extension

- Change teams to 4 v 3.
- Use football/hockey equipment, adding an extra skittle to make a goal.

Full Activity Description

The aim of the game is to score points by bouncing the ball in a target hoop or knocking over a target skittle.

Place a hoop or skittle in a target circle about 2–3m across. The playing space extends all around this circle, but players are not allowed to enter the circle. Play the game 4 v 2 and, later, 4 v 3. Both teams score by hitting the target hoop or skittle. After a 'goal', the larger team takes a free pass from a specific starting point away from the circle. Both teams can travel with the ball by bouncing it. There is no physical contact.

SCORE IN YOUR GOAL

Activity 2, Upper Key Stage 1/Lower to Middle Key Stage 2 (Age 7–9)

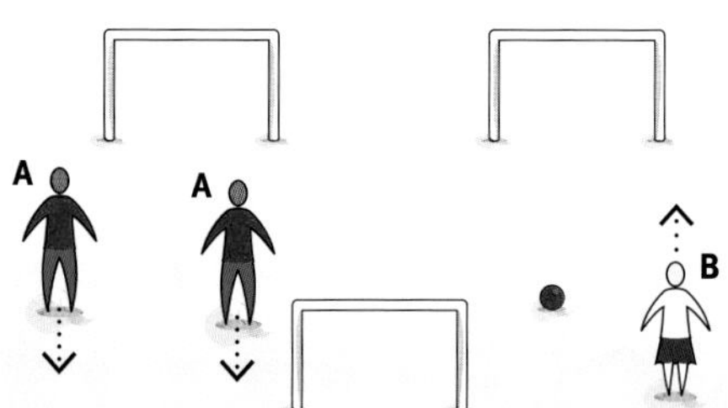

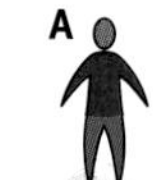

1 Person **A:** Do not move with the ball.

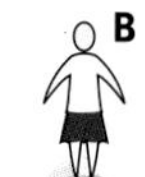

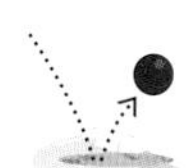

2 Person **B:** Only bounce or dribble the ball.

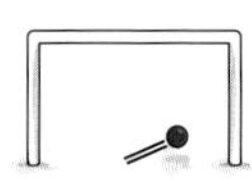

3 Person **A:** Restart from your goal line.

LEADER NOTES

Objectives

Pupils should:

- be able to attempt to attack and defend in a game situation
- know and understand the term 'dribble'
- continue to develop fundamental movement skills and become increasingly competent and confident
- apply and develop a broader range of skills, learning how to use them in different ways
- be able to engage in competitive and cooperative physical activities in a range of increasingly challenging situations, and enjoy communicating, collaborating and competing with each other
- start to develop an understanding of how to improve, and learn how to evaluate and recognise their own success.

Differentiation and Extension

Easier

- Give the smaller team a timed start advantage.
- Play 3 v 2.

Harder

- Increase the number of goals.
- Play with non-dominant hand/foot.

Extension

- Move the goals to different positions around the pitch.
- Play on a longer, thinner pitch.

Full Activity Description

The aim of the game is to score more goals than the opposition. Play using throwing and catching skills, kicking skills or striking skills. Select appropriate equipment for the game.

Play this end-to-end game on a pitch that is about 10m x 20m (wider than it is long). Play 3 v 1 and, later, 3 v 2.Put 3 small goals at 1 end of the pitch (for the team of 3) and 1 large goal at the other end. The larger team is not allowed to travel with the ball, but the smaller team is allowed to travel by bouncing (or dribbling) the ball. There is no physical contact. The team of 3 takes all restart passes from its own goal line after a goal has been scored or the ball goes out of play.

SCORE FROM INSIDE THE END ZONE

Activity 3, Middle Key Stage 2 (Age 8–9)

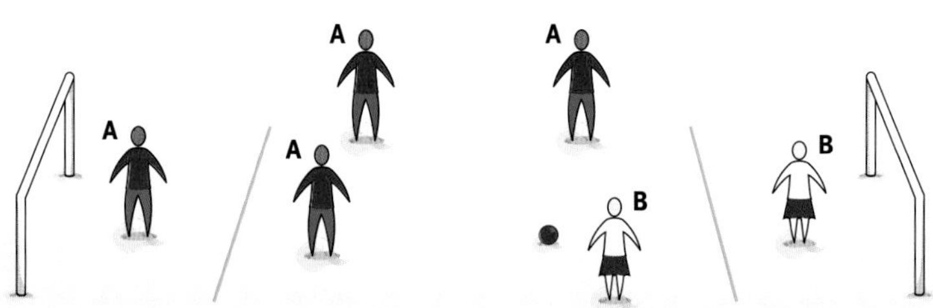

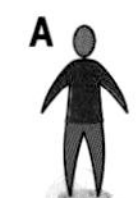

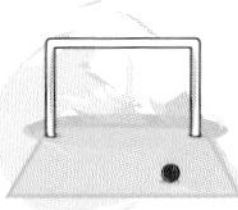

1 Person **A:** Pass the ball to another **A** in the end zone.

Person **A:** Stop the ball and score.

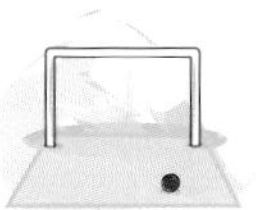

2 End zone person **A** can move anywhere.

3 **Restart** from the **opposite** team goal line.

LEADER NOTES

Objectives

Pupils should:

- be able to move to the correct position in order to attempt to score
- know and understand that, in some games, you have to be in a certain position to attempt to score
- continue to apply and develop a broader range of skills, learning how to use them in different ways and linking them to make actions
- enjoy communicating, collaborating and competing with each other
- start to develop an understanding of how to improve, and learn how to evaluate and recognise their own success.

Differentiation and Extension

Easier

- Use only throwing and catching, no travelling.
- Play in smaller teams.

Harder

- Play 4 v 3.
- Play in a smaller area.

Extension

- Use non-typical equipment (eg Frisbee).
- Change the goal to a hoop.

Full Activity Description

The aim of the game is to pass the ball to a nominated player in the end zone of a pitch.

Play the game 4 v 2 and then 4 v 3. Play on a pitch that is about 10m x 20m. The end zones should be about 1m wide, running the width of the pitch. Use netball, basketball, football or hockey equipment and techniques.

To score points, the ball has to be passed to, and stopped by, a player who has been nominated to receive the ball in the end zone. This player can move anywhere on the pitch, but must be in the end zone to receive the ball and then shoot to score a 'goal'. The goals can be hoops, nets, posts etc. After every goal, the team that did not score takes a free pass from its back line. If the ball goes out, the opposition throws in from where the ball went out.

SCORE IN THE GOAL WITH THE HIGHEST POINTS

Activity 4, Middle Key Stage 2 (Age 8–9)

1 Person **A:** Pass the ball to another **A** in the end zone.

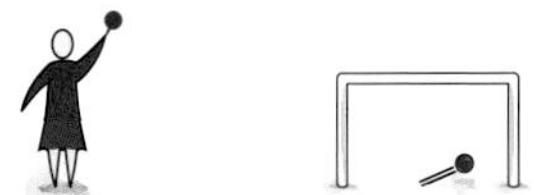

Person **A:** Stop the ball and score.

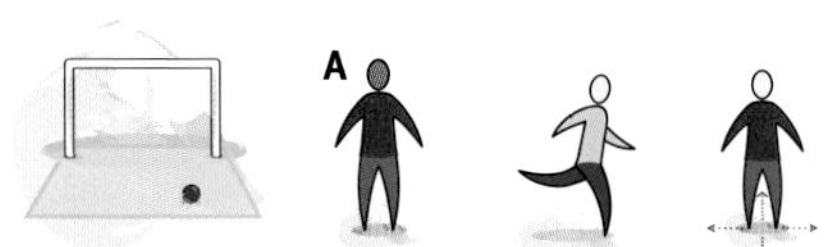

2 End zone Person **A** can move anywhere.

3 **Middle** goal = **3** points. **Side** goals = **1** point.

LEADER NOTES

Objectives

Pupils should:

- be able to choose priority/danger areas that should be defended
- know and understand that some areas should be defended more carefully within a game
- continue to apply and develop a broader range of skills, learning how to use them in different ways and linking them to make actions
- enjoy communicating, collaborating and competing with each other
- start to develop an understanding of how to improve, and learn how to evaluate and recognise their own success.

Differentiation and Extension

Easier

- Use more goals.
- Award a free shot/pass after a ball has been received in the end zone.
- Allow any player to score.

Harder

- Play 3 v 3.
- Play on a smaller playing area.

Extension

- Move the goals into the playing area.
- Allow shooting from all angles.

Full Activity Description

The aim of the game is to pass the ball to a nominated player standing in 1 of the targets at the end of the playing space.

Play 3 v 2 and then 3 v 3. Play on a pitch that is about 10m x 20m and position 3 goals at either end of the pitch. Follow similar rules to those described in Activity 3. Each team has 3 goals to score in – the middle goal is worth 3 points; the outer goals are worth 1. Start by using throwing and catching skills, then introduce equipment and rules using kicking or striking skills.

THINK OF YOUR OWN GAME

Activity 5, Middle Key Stage 2 (Age 8–9)

1 Choose equipment for your game.

2 Choose rules and how players will score.

3 Choose how to start and how to keep safe.

LEADER NOTES

Objectives

Pupils should:

- be able to agree and teach the rules of their new game
- know and understand the importance of making a game as safe as possible
- continue to apply and develop a broader range of skills, learning how to use them in different ways and linking them to make actions
- enjoy communicating, collaborating and competing with each other
- start to develop an understanding of how to improve, and learn how to evaluate and recognise their own success.

Differentiation and Extension

Easier

- Provide some visual examples of changes to a well-known game.
- Place all available equipment on show.

Harder

- Place in randomly assigned groups.
- Assign specific equipment to groups.

Extension

- Teach the game to other groups/the rest of the class.
- Explore safety with 'what if' scenarios.

Full Activity Description

Ask the children to make up their own invasion game and find ways to play it well. Ask them to choose:

- rules
- equipment
- how to score
- how to start and restart the game.

Tell them to think about how to make sure their game is safe to play.

SCORE THE MOST GOALS

Activity 6, Middle to Upper Key Stage 2 (Age 9–11)

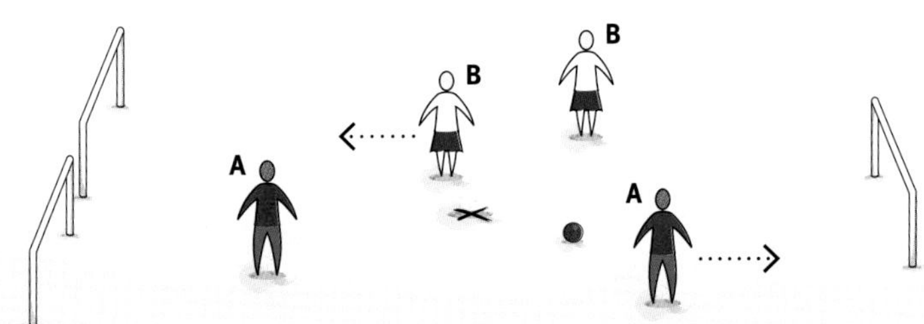

1 Score in your goal with **no** goalkeeper.

2 **Restart** the game between the **2** goals.

››› LEADER NOTES

Objectives

Pupils should:

- be able to pass to players who are in a position to shoot at goal
- know and understand that players must pass to others to increase the chances of scoring goals
- continue to apply and develop a broader range of skills, learning how to use them in different ways
- enjoy communicating, collaborating and competing with each other
- develop an understanding of how to improve in different physical activities and sports, and learn how to evaluate and recognise their own success.

Differentiation and Extension

Easier

- Use fewer defenders.
- Increase the size of the playing area.

Harder

- Play 5 v 4.
- Decrease the size of the playing area.

Extension

- Focus on different invasion games.
- Focus on rugby, using 'try hoops' along the back lines.

Full Activity Description

The aim of the game is to beat the opposition by scoring more goals.

Play the game 5 v 3 and then 5 v 4. Play on a pitch that is 20–30m wide and 30–40m long. Position 1 large goal at 1 end of the pitch and 2 smaller goals at the other end. Use netball, basketball, hockey or football equipment and skills. Make the pitch smaller if you choose to focus on netball skills.

The team with 5 players attacks the large goal while the team with fewer players attacks the 2 smaller goals. There are no goalkeepers. After each goal, and whenever the ball goes out of play, the larger team starts with a free pass from the line between the goals it is defending.

PASS AND SCORE A GOAL

Activity 7, Middle to Upper Key Stage 2 (Age 9–11)

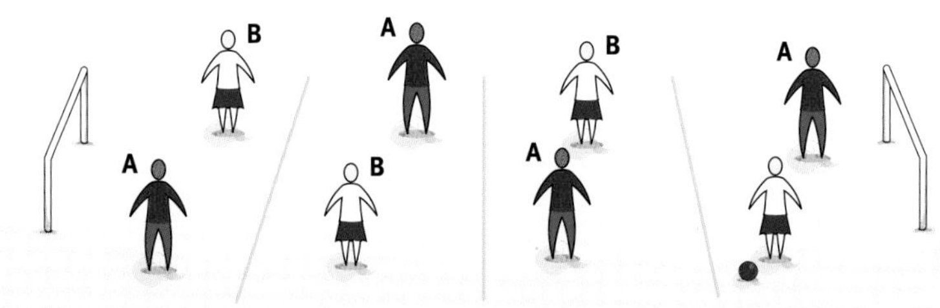

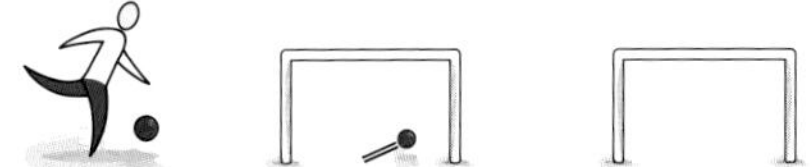

1 Score in your goal with **no** goalkeeper.

2 Do not pass the ball over **2 lines**.

3 Do not dribble the ball over **2 sections**.

Objectives

Pupils should:

- be able to pass to players who are in a position to shoot at goal
- know and understand that players must pass to others to increase the chances of scoring goals
- continue to apply and develop a broader range of skills, learning how to use them in different ways
- enjoy communicating, collaborating and competing with each other
- develop an understanding of how to improve in different physical activities and sports, and learn how to evaluate and recognise their own success.

Differentiation and Extension

Easier

- Use fewer defenders.
- Increase the size of the playing area.

Harder

- Play 5 v 5.
- Decrease the size of the playing area.

Extension

- Play with large goals and goalkeepers.

Full Activity Description

The aim of the game is to beat the opposition by scoring more goals.

Play 5 v 4 and then 5 v 5. Play on a pitch that is about 20m x 40m, divided into 4 sections with a goal at either end. Use mini-hockey or mini-football rules, and play the game with small goals and no goalkeepers or larger goals with keepers. Players must not pass the ball over more than 2 lines or dribble the ball across a line between sections. There is no limit on where they can go.

SCORE A GOAL FROM INSIDE THE SHOOTING AREA

Activity 8, Upper Key Stage 2 (Age 10–11)

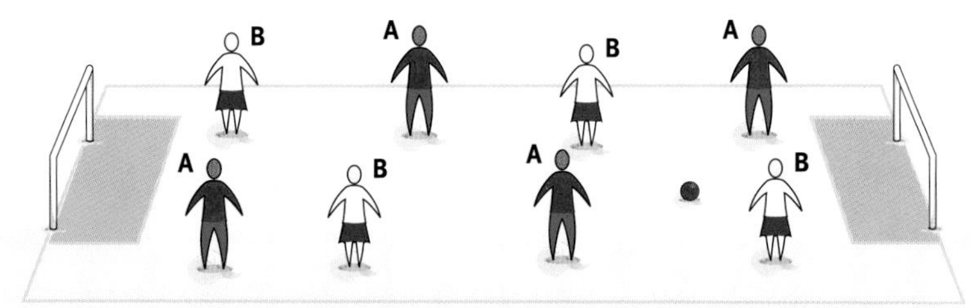

  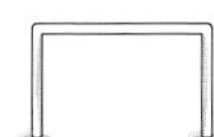

1 Shoot only in the scoring area, with **no** goalkeeper.

2 Organise your team to attack and defend **well**.

LEADER NOTES

Objectives

Pupils should:

- be able to describe an attacking position and a defending position within a game situation
- know and understand positions that help attacking and defending positions within a game
- apply and develop a broader range of skills, using them in different ways and linking them to make actions and sequences of movement
- enjoy communicating, collaborating and competing with each other
- develop an understanding of how to improve in different physical activities and sports, and learn how to evaluate and recognise their own success.

Differentiation and Extension

Easier

- Only allow attackers in the shooting area with 1 defender or no person.
- Play with uneven teams.

Harder

- Play 5 v 5.
- Play with a larger shooting area/smaller goals.
- Allow limited players only to shoot/limited touches per player.

Extension

- Use bibs to differentiate attackers/defenders and explore player roles.

Full Activity Description

The aim of the game is to beat the opposition by scoring more goals.

Play the game 4 v 4 and then 5 v 5. Play on a pitch that is 15–20m wide and 30–40m long. Position 1 goal at each end of the pitch, with a shooting area of about 10m x 10m.

At first, play without goalkeepers and only allow players to shoot when they are in the shooting area.

Later, allow players to shoot from outside the area, and add goalkeepers. Encourage teams to think about how they need to change the way they organise themselves to attack and defend in the different games.

ATTACK AND DEFEND TO SCORE A GOAL

Activity 9, Upper Key Stage 2 (Age 10–11)

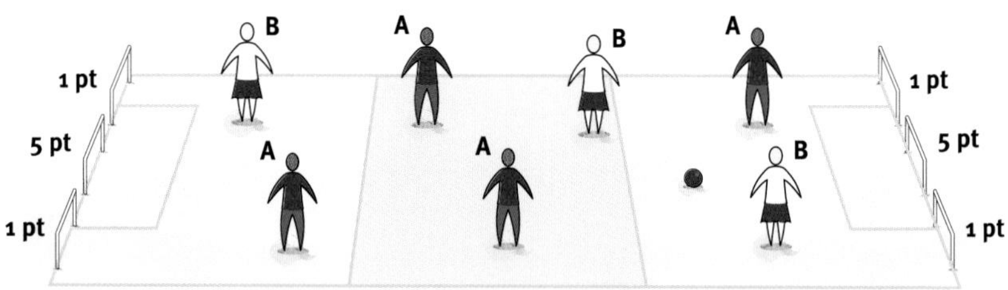

1 No tackling in the **middle** zone.

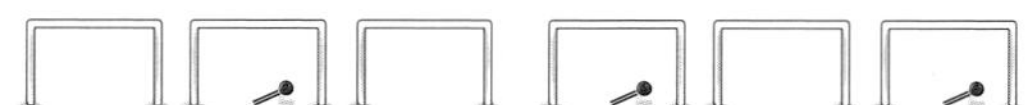

2 **Middle** goal = **5** points. **Side** goals = **1** point.

3 Choose ways to attack and defend.

LEADER NOTES

Objectives

Pupils should:

- be able to attempt to intercept
- know and understand the term 'intercept'
- apply and develop a broader range of skills, using them in different ways and linking them to make actions and sequences of movement
- enjoy communicating, collaborating and competing with each other
- develop an understanding of how to improve in different physical activities and sports, and learn how to evaluate and recognise their own success.

Differentiation and Extension

Easier

- Play with larger/more goals.
- Play with uneven teams.

Harder

- Play 5 v 5.
- Only allow particular players into certain sections.

Extension

- Change the sizes of the sections.
- Use rugby rules with 6 scoring markers.

Full Activity Description

The aim of the game is to beat the opposition by scoring more goals.

Play the game 4 v 4 and then 5 v 5. Play on a pitch that is about 30m x 40m, divided into 3 areas. Position 3 goals at each end of the pitch. Use football or hockey rules.

The game is played in a similar way to Activity 8. Players are not allowed to tackle in the middle third of the pitch, but may intercept the ball. The middle goal at each end is worth 5 points, and the outer goals are worth 1 point. Encourage the children to think about the different ways they can attack and defend.

»» PLAY A 5-A-SIDE GAME

Activity 10, Upper Key Stage 2 (Age 10–11)

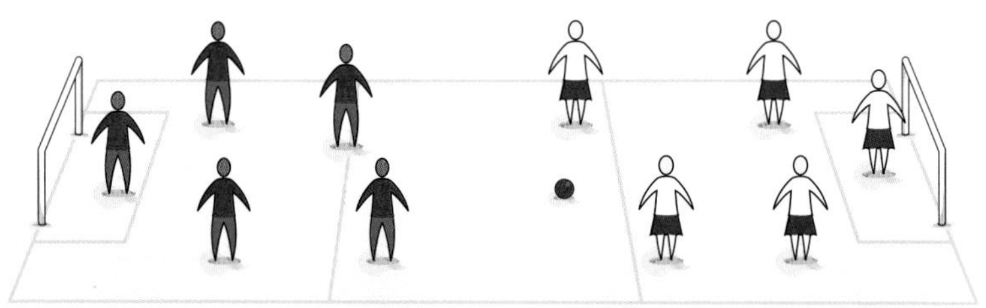

1 Choose a **5**-a-side game to play.

LEADER NOTES

Objectives

Pupils should:

- be able to play a 5-a-side game
- know and understand games that are suitable to play in 5-a-side teams
- apply and develop a broader range of skills, using them in different ways and linking them to make actions and sequences of movement
- enjoy communicating, collaborating and competing with each other
- develop an understanding of how to improve in different physical activities and sports, and learn how to evaluate and recognise their own success.

Differentiation and Extension

Easier

- Dictate the game to play and playing area to play on.
- Dictate rules to suit the adapted game(s).

Harder

- Get the group to determine rules for the adapted game(s).
- Get the group to determine the game to play and pitch size to play on.

Extension

- Vary team and pitch sizes.
- Investigate how to make other games suitable for 5-a-side play.

Full Activity Description

Play 5 v 5 versions of mini-football, mini-hockey, mini-rugby, mini-netball or mini-basketball.

SCORE GOALS, STAYING OUT OF THE SAFE ZONE

Activity 11, Upper Key Stage 2/Key Stage 3 (Age 10–14)

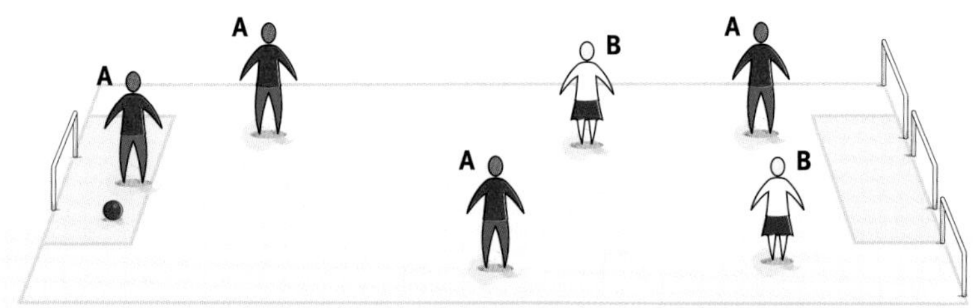

1 Attackers start with the ball in the safe zone near their own goal.

2 Attackers try to score in 1 of 3 goals.

3 Attackers restart after each goal.

LEADER NOTES

Objectives

Pupils should:

- be able to identify and stay out of the opposition's safe zone
- know and understand the purpose of a safe zone
- continue to implement and develop a broader range of skills, learning how to use them in different ways
- enjoy communicating, collaborating and competing with each other
- develop an understanding of how to succeed in different activities and sports, and learn how to evaluate and recognise their own success
- understand what makes a performance effective and apply these principles to their own and others' work
- become more competent, confident and expert in their techniques, and apply them across different sports and activities
- develop the confidence and interest to get involved in exercise, sports and activities outside school.

Differentiation and Extension

Easier

- Play with larger/more goals.
- Play with uneven teams.
- Play from inside a zone in front of a target.

Harder

- Play 4 v 3.
- Play with goals on the playing area, allowing shooting from all directions.
- Rule that the ball should pass through a number of zones before attempting to score.

Extension

- Play a variety of invasion games – water polo, hockey, netball, football etc.

Full Activity Description

Play with 4 attackers v 2defenders (progress to 4 v 3). Attackers start with the ball from a safe exclusion zone near their own goal. They attempt to score in 1 of 3 goals. Defenders can score in 1 large goal, shooting from outside the exclusion zone. After each goal, the attackers restart from the exclusion zone.

GAIN POSSESSION AND SCORE A GOAL

Activity 12, Upper Key Stage 2/Key Stage 3 (Age 10–14)

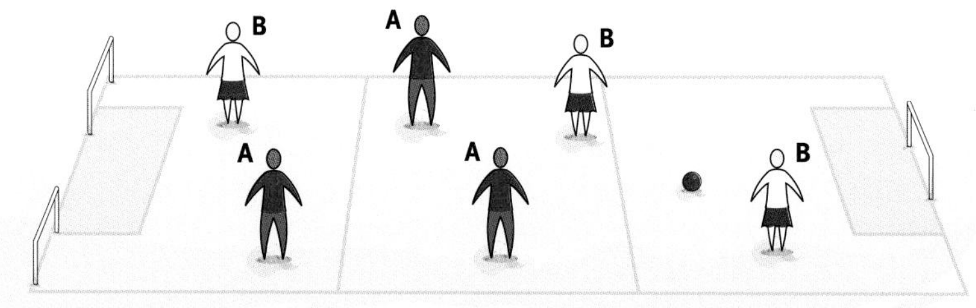

1 Attackers start with the ball in their third of the pitch.

2 Attackers try to score in the defenders' goal.

3 Defenders try to gain possession and score in 1 of the goals at the wings.

LEADER NOTES

Objectives

Pupils should:

- be able to attempt to gain possession
- know and understand the term 'to gain possession'
- continue to implement and develop a broader range of skills, learning how to use them in different ways
- enjoy communicating, collaborating and competing with each other
- develop an understanding of how to succeed in different activities and sports, and learn how to evaluate and recognise their own success
- understand what makes a performance effective and apply these principles to their own and others' work
- become more competent, confident and expert in their techniques, and apply them across different sports and activities
- develop the confidence and interest to get involved in exercise, sports and activities outside school.

Differentiation and Extension

Easier

- Play with larger/more goals.
- Play with uneven teams.
- Play from inside a zone in front of a target.

Harder

- Play 3 v 4.
- Play with goals on the playing area, allowing shooting from all directions.
- Rule that the ball should pass through a number of zones before attempting to score.

Extension

- Play a variety of invasion games – water polo, hockey, netball, football etc.

Full Activity Description

Play with 3 attackers v 3 defenders (progress to 4 defenders). Attackers start with the ball in their own third of the pitch and try to score in the defenders' goal. The defenders attempt to 'gain' possession and score in 1 of 2 goals, wide on the wings of the pitch.

PLAN A GAME TO SHOW EFFECTIVE TEAM PLAY

Activity 13, Upper Key Stage 2/Key Stage 3 (Age 10–14)

1 Plan your game, thinking of:

- effective team play
- applying tactics.

2 Think about the principles of:

- attack
- defence
- transpossession.

Objectives

Pupils should:

- be able to discuss a game plan before playing
- know and understand the term 'transpossession'
- continue to implement and develop a broader range of skills, learning how to use them in different ways
- enjoy communicating, collaborating and competing with each other
- develop an understanding of how to succeed in different activities and sports, and learn how to evaluate and recognise their own success
- understand what makes a performance effective and apply these principles to their own and others' work
- become more competent, confident and expert in their techniques, and apply them across different sports and activities
- develop the confidence and interest to get involved in exercise, sports and activities outside school.

Differentiation and Extension

Easier

- Play with larger/more goals.
- Play with uneven teams.
- Play from inside a zone in front of a target.

Harder

- Play 3 v 4.
- Play with goals on the playing area, allowing shooting from all directions.
- Rule that the ball should pass through a number of zones before attempting to score.

Extension

- Play a variety of invasion games – water polo, hockey, netball, football etc.

Full Activity Description

In small-sided versions of the games (4 v 4, 5 v 5, 6 v 6 or 7 v 7), pupils plan for effective team play, applying tactics with an understanding of the principles of attack, defence and transpossession.

›››

STRIKING AND FIELDING GAMES

HIT THE BALL AND JUMP INTO THE HOOP UNTIL THE BALL IS RETURNED

Activity 1, Upper Key Stage 1/Lower to Middle Key Stage 2 (Age 7–9)

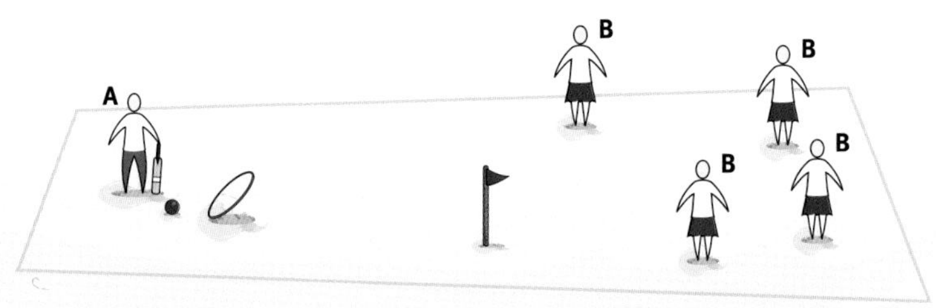

1 Person **A:** Hit the ball off a low tee.

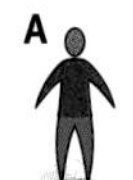

2 Person **A:** Quickly jump into and out of the hoop

before the ball is **returned**.

3 Person **B:** Pass the ball to each fielder

and quickly return the ball to base.

>>> LEADER NOTES

Objectives

Pupils should:

- be able to pass and catch within a small team
- know and understand how a batting turn is completed once a ball is returned to base
- continue to develop fundamental movement skills and become increasingly competent and confident
- apply and develop a broader range of skills, learning how to use them in different ways
- be able to engage in competitive and cooperative physical activities in a range of increasingly challenging situations, and enjoy communicating, collaborating and competing with each other
- start to develop an understanding of how to improve, and learn how to evaluate and recognise their own success.

Differentiation and Extension

Easier

- Throw/roll the ball.
- Work in batting pairs – 1 player bats, the other jumps/runs.

Harder

- Play 3 v 1.
- Introduce a bowler.

Extension

- Run around bases instead of jumping into/out of a hoop.
- Delegate roles to players (eg wicketkeeper, bowler, fielder, batter).

Full Activity Description

The aim of the game is for the batter to hit the ball in an arc and score points by jumping into and out of a hoop, or bouncing a ball, as many times as possible before the fielding team returns the ball to base.

Play the game 3 v 1 or 4 v 1. The batter hits the ball off a low tee in an arc. The players field the ball and then pass it to each other. When all the fielders have touched the ball, the batter stops scoring. Change around after 4–5 strikes. Encourage the children to keep their own scores and try to beat their last score the next time they bat.

HIT THE BALL AND RUN UNTIL THE BALL IS RETURNED

Activity 2, Upper Key Stage 1/Lower to Middle Key Stage 2 (Age 7–9)

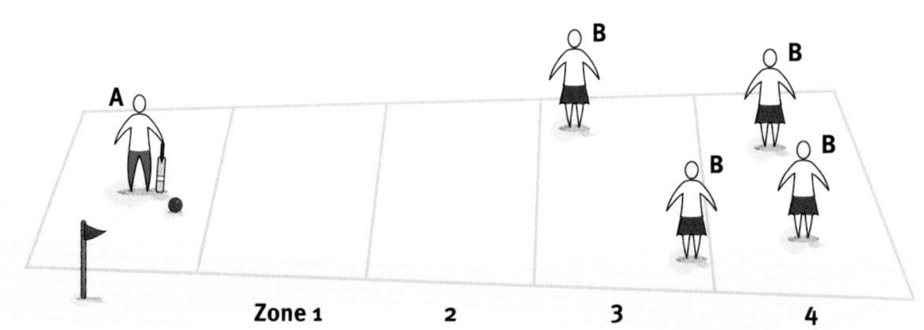

1 Person **A**: Hit the ball off a low tee.

2 Person **A**: Run to 1 of the 4 zones.

3 Person **B**: Quickly return the ball to base

before Person **A** returns.

>>> LEADER NOTES

Objectives

Pupils should:

- be able to bat and run to distant bases
- know and understand how hitting the ball further increases the chance of running further distances
- continue to develop fundamental movement skills and become increasingly competent and confident
- apply and develop a broader range of skills, learning how to use them in different ways
- be able to engage in competitive and cooperative physical activities in a range of increasingly challenging situations, and enjoy communicating, collaborating and competing with each other
- start to develop an understanding of how to improve, and learn how to evaluate and recognise their own success.

Differentiation and Extension

Easier

- Throw/roll the ball.
- Work in batting pairs – 1 player bats, the other runs.

Harder

- Play 3 v 1.
- Introduce a bowler.

Extension

- Place bases to run to/around.
- Delegate roles to players (eg wicketkeeper, bowler, fielder, batter).

Full Activity Description

The aim of this game is to hit the ball in an arc and score points by running to 1 of 4 zones before the fielding team gets the ball back to the stumping base.

Play the game 3 v 1 or 4 v 1. The batter hits the ball off a low tee in an arc and runs to 1 of the 4 zones. The fielders retrieve the ball and try to get it back to the stumping base as quickly as possible. Each player should have 4–5 goes at hitting before the next 1 has a turn. Add up the scores for each hit to make an innings score.

THINK OF YOUR OWN GAME

Activity 3, Upper Key Stage 1/Lower to Middle Key Stage 2 (Age 7–9)

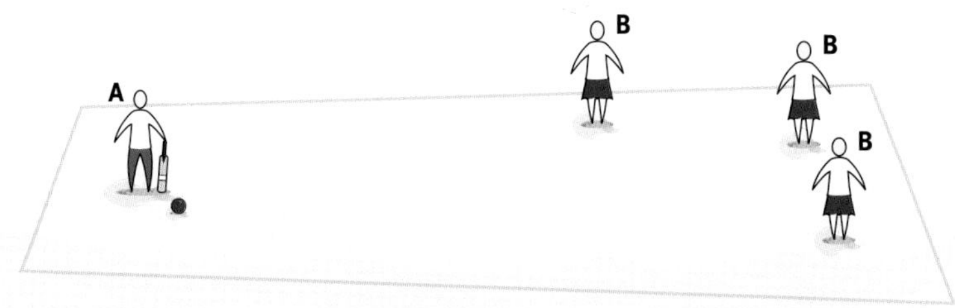

1 Choose a new game to teach to friends.

2-1

2 Choose a good scoring **system** for your game.

3 What would you **change** in your game?

>>> LEADER NOTES

Objectives

Pupils should:

- be able to teach friends their new game
- know and understand how to score points in their new game
- continue to develop fundamental movement skills and become increasingly competent and confident
- apply and develop a broader range of skills, learning how to use them in different ways
- be able to engage in competitive and cooperative physical activities in a range of increasingly challenging situations, and enjoy communicating, collaborating and competing with each other
- start to develop an understanding of how to improve, and learn how to evaluate and recognise their own success.

Differentiation and Extension

Easier

- Ask leading questions such as 'Which part of the game would you like to change/do you not like?'
- Place all available equipment on show.

Harder

- Place pupils in randomly assigned groups.

Extension

- Teach the game to other groups/the rest of the class.

Full Activity Description

Ask the children to adapt the rules, equipment or skills of the game they are playing so it suits them better. Then ask them to make up a new striking and fielding game with a scoring system. They should be able to play their game well and teach it to others in the class.

HIT THE BALL AND RUN BETWEEN THE WICKETS

Activity 4, Middle to Upper Key Stage 2 (Age 9–11)

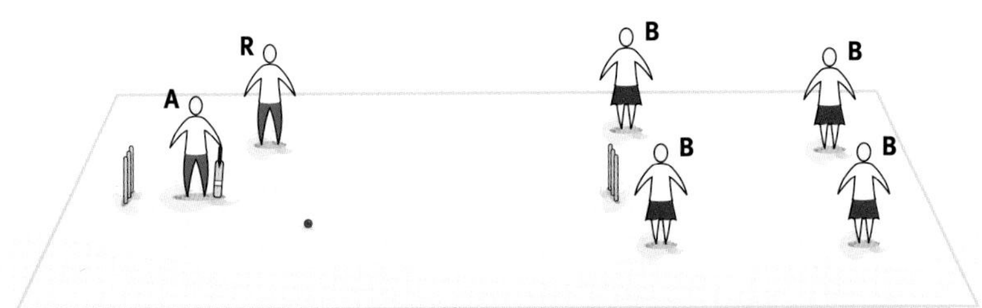

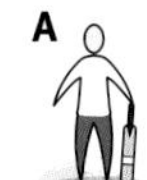

1 Person **A:** Hit the ball. Person **R:** Run

to the wicket and back = **1** run.

2 If the ball is caught or lands at base, do not run.

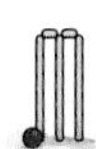

3 Person **A:** Change wickets after **6** balls.

Person **A** and Person **R:** Change after **12** balls.

››› LEADER NOTES

Objectives

Pupils should:

- be able to hit a ball and run between 2 wickets
- know and understand the term 'run' and how to score a run
- continue to apply and develop a broader range of skills, learning how to use them in different ways
- enjoy communicating, collaborating and competing with each other
- develop an understanding of how to improve in different physical activities and sports, and learn how to evaluate and recognise their own success.

Differentiation and Extension

Easier

- Hit from a tee.
- Hit into a larger area.

Harder

- Place wickets further apart.
- Hit into a smaller area.

Extension

- Introduce tactics (eg attempting to bowl the batter out).
- Run around bases set around circuit, and award points for bases reached.

Full Activity Description

The aim of this game is for a pair (1 batter and 1 runner) to score as many runs as possible.

Play the game 2 v 4. 1 of the pair bats while the other runs. The batter is only allowed to hit the ball into 1 area of the field. Once the batter has hit the ball, the runner runs between 2 wickets or bases, scoring 1 run for getting there and back. The runner is not allowed to run if the fielders have caught the ball before it hits the ground or after the fielders have got the ball back to the return base.

After 6 balls, the batter swaps ends but still hits into the same area of the field. After 12 balls, the runner and batter change roles. The fielders take it in turns to bowl and must try to stop the pair scoring.

››› PLAY AN INNINGS AS PART OF A PAIR

Activity 5, Middle to Upper Key Stage 2 (Age 9–11)

1 Get into **3** pairs: batters, fielders

and bowler and wicketkeeper.

2 Share **3, 6, 9** or **12** bowls over a **12-** or **24-**ball innings.

3 In the beginning, you have **10** runs.

  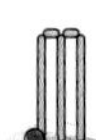 

If caught, run or bowled out, lose **5** runs.

>>> LEADER NOTES

Objectives

Pupils should:

- be able to play a predetermined cricket innings
- know and understand the term 'innings'
- continue to apply and develop a broader range of skills, learning how to use them in different ways
- enjoy communicating, collaborating and competing with each other
- develop an understanding of how to improve in different physical activities and sports, and learn how to evaluate and recognise their own success.

Differentiation and Extension

Easier

- Award 'lives' to batters.
- Award bonus points for technique.

Harder

- Enforce the rule 'the whole batting team is out' if caught/run/bowled out.
- Use overarm bowling.

Extension

- Play in 360° arc.

Full Activity Description

The aim of this game is for pairs to score as many runs as possible in an innings of a set length.

Start with a 3-pair game: 1 pair bats; 1 pair fields; and the third pair bowls and keeps wicket. The bowling pair takes it in turns to bowl from either end (3, 6 or 12 balls each). Set a length for an innings (eg 12 or 24 balls). At the end of an innings, the pairs swap roles. Each pair starts with 10 runs, which they add to when batting by running or scoring boundaries. They lose 5 runs when they are run out, caught or bowled.

»» SCORE AS MANY POINTS AS YOU CAN IN YOUR INNINGS

Activity 6, Upper Key Stage 2/Key Stage 3 (Age 10–14)

1 The batter and bowler play on the same team, sharing 6 bowls each against 6 fielders.

2 Points are scored by runs and lost when a player becomes out.

3 The batting team should be preset a number of points to achieve.

LEADER NOTES

Objectives

Pupils should:

- be able to bowl for a team player to readily attempt to hit the ball
- know and understand that, in cricket, multiple fielders attempt to stop the batter's play
- continue to implement and develop a broader range of skills, learning how to use them in different ways
- enjoy communicating, collaborating and competing with each other
- develop an understanding of how to succeed in different activities and sports, and learn how to evaluate and recognise their own success
- understand what makes a performance effective and apply these principles to their own and others' work
- become more competent, confident and expert in their techniques, and apply them across different sports and activities
- develop the confidence and interest to get involved in exercise, sports and activities outside school.

Differentiation and Extension

Easier

- Use lighter bats/bats with a larger surface area.
- Use a hitting tee.

Harder

- Set specific areas for batters to hit into.
- Use cricket/rounders balls.

Extension

- Play in a 360° arc.

Full Activity Description

The purpose of this game is for the batting pair to score as many runs as they can in their innings. In each group, pupils should play 6 fielders against the team of bowler and batter working together.

The bowler and batter have 12 deliveries (6 each) during which they should score as many runs/points as possible. Points are scored either by running round the bases (eg softball or rounders) or between wickets (eg stoolball or cricket). They should decide on which rules they will play to. The batting pair should set, or be set, a target of points/runs to achieve. If either of them is out, they will lose a point/run.

BEAT THE BATTING OR BOWLING PAIR BY GETTING THE MOST POINTS

Activity 7, Upper Key Stage 2/Key Stage 3 (Age 10–14)

1 Points are awarded for each:

- completed run
- time a post/wicket is passed
- time a wicket is taken/batter is out.

2 Bowlers are supported by 4 fielders.

3 Innings are made up of 20–30 balls.

»» LEADER NOTES

Objectives

Pupils should:

- be able to score points by hitting a ball and running safely to the target
- know and understand that it is advantageous to attempt to field a batter 'out'
- continue to implement and develop a broader range of skills, learning how to use them in different ways
- enjoy communicating, collaborating and competing with each other
- develop an understanding of how to succeed in different activities and sports, and learn how to evaluate and recognise their own success
- understand what makes a performance effective and apply these principles to their own and others' work
- become more competent, confident and expert in their techniques, and apply them across different sports and activities
- develop the confidence and interest to get involved in exercise, sports and activities outside school.

Differentiation and Extension

Easier

- Bowl from a closer proximity.
- Give a 3-second delay until fielders can react after a ball is hit.

Harder

- Set targets of points to attempt to achieve.
- Award bonus points to fielders who 'assist' in getting the batter out.

Extension

- Play in a 360° arc.

Full Activity Description

The purpose of the game is for a batting pair to play against a bowling pair and see who can score the most points. Points are scored for each completed run, each time a post is passed, and each time a wicket is taken or a batter would be given out in a full game. 4 other fielders support the bowlers. Each innings should be 20–30 balls. At the end of the innings, the bowling pair bat against the batting pair. Each pair tries to add to their score. At the end of this 'match', the fielders form 2 pairs and play their match.

NET/WALL GAMES

PUSH THE BALL OVER THE LINE

Activity 1, Upper Key Stage 1/Lower to Middle Key Stage 2 (Age 7–9)

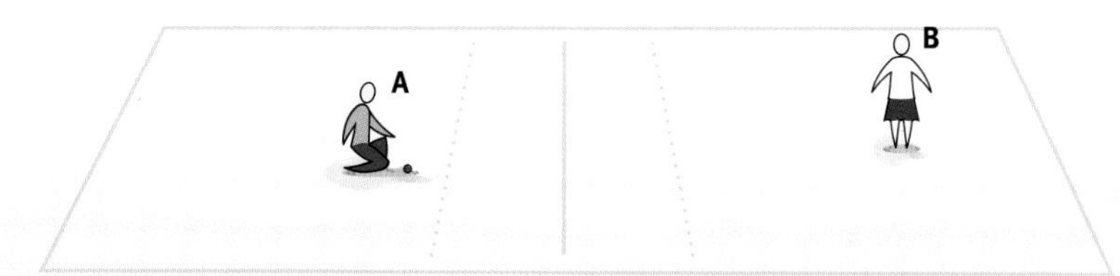

1 Do not cross the line.

2 Person **A:** Push the ball over the line.

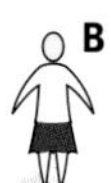

3 Person **B:** Stop the ball crossing the line.

LEADER NOTES

Objectives

Pupils should:

- be able to defend an area
- know and understand how to position themselves to make defending easier
- continue to develop fundamental movement skills and become increasingly competent and confident
- apply and develop a broader range of skills, learning how to use them in different ways
- be able to engage in competitive and cooperative physical activities in a range of increasingly challenging situations, and enjoy communicating, collaborating and competing with each other
- start to develop an understanding of how to improve, and learn how to evaluate and recognise their own success.

Differentiation and Extension

Easier

- Use a large ball.
- Stand close to the line.

Harder

- Move the lines further apart.
- Use smaller/more balls.
- Use non-dominant hand.

Extension

- Bounce the ball(s).
- Use a net.

Full Activity Description

The aim of the game is to score points by throwing a ball into the opponent's court area and making it bounce twice.

Play the game 1 v 1. Use a low net (bench to short tennis height) on a court that is relatively long and narrow. Put a gym mat on either side of the net, about 1m away from the net, and make the court a little larger than this. Use throwing and catching skills.

Once the children can play the game confidently, move on to introduce hitting the ball with a racket after it has bounced. A partner playing with the hitter should feed the ball. Try adapting the rules so the partner has to catch the ball before feeding it to be hit. More able players will be able to rally without a partner feeding the ball. They may need more than 1 bounce.

This game is easiest with a big ball that bounces well. It can also be played by pushing or sliding the ball across a line that is being defended. (This is easier for some children who have difficulties with coordination.)

THROW THE BALL AND MAKE IT BOUNCE TWICE

Activity 2, Upper Key Stage 1/Lower to Middle Key Stage 2 (Age 7–9)

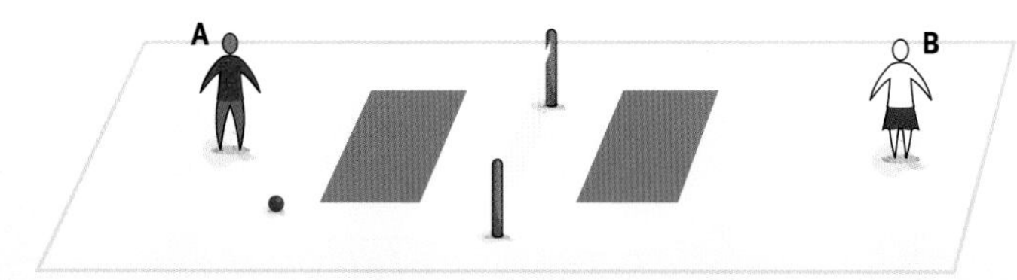

1 Throw the ball over the net.

2 Make the ball land past the mat.

3 Make the ball bounce on the opposite side of the court twice.

LEADER NOTES

Objectives

Pupils should:

- be able to throw a ball over a net
- know and understand how to throw balls high and at a distance
- continue to develop fundamental movement skills and become increasingly competent and confident
- apply and develop a broader range of skills, learning how to use them in different ways
- be able to engage in competitive and cooperative physical activities in a range of increasingly challenging situations, and enjoy communicating, collaborating and competing with each other
- start to develop an understanding of how to improve, and learn how to evaluate and recognise their own success.

Differentiation and Extension

Easier

- Use a large ball.
- Stand closer to the net/on the mat.

Harder

- Play on a larger court.
- Use a higher net.
- Move the mats further from the net.

Extension

- Increase the numbers of players.

Full Activity Description

The aim of the game is to score points by throwing a ball into the opponent's court area and making it bounce twice.

Play the game 1 v 1. Use a low net (bench to short tennis height) on a court that is relatively long and narrow. Put a gym mat on either side of the net, about 1m away from the net, and make the court a little larger than this. Use throwing and catching skills.

Once the children can play the game confidently, move on to introduce hitting the ball with a racket after it has bounced. A partner playing with the hitter should feed the ball. Try adapting the rules so the partner has to catch the ball before feeding it to be hit. More able players will be able to rally without a partner feeding the ball. They may need more than 1 bounce.

This game is easiest with a big ball that bounces well. It can also be played by pushing or sliding the ball across a line that is being defended. (This is easier for some children who have difficulties with coordination.)

WATCH THE BALL BOUNCE AND HIT IT BACK

Activity 3, Upper Key Stage 1/Lower to Middle Key Stage 2 (Age 7–9)

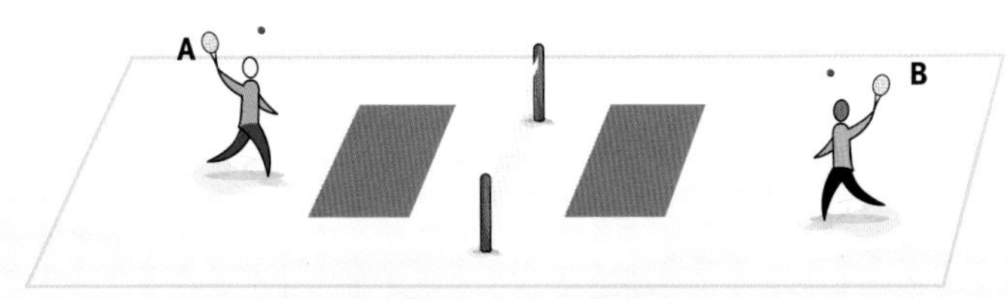

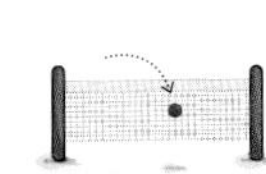

1 Ask a partner to throw the ball over the net.

2 Watch the ball bounce on your side of the court

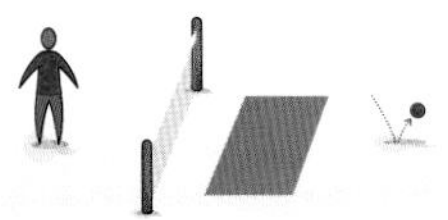

past the mat.

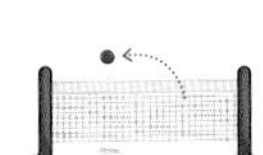

3 Hit the ball back over the net.

LEADER NOTES

Objectives

Pupils should:

- be able to throw a ball over a net
- know and understand how to throw balls high and at a distance
- continue to develop fundamental movement skills and become increasingly competent and confident
- apply and develop a broader range of skills, learning how to use them in different ways
- be able to engage in competitive and cooperative physical activities in a range of increasingly challenging situations, and enjoy communicating, collaborating and competing with each other
- start to develop an understanding of how to improve, and learn how to evaluate and recognise their own success.

Differentiation and Extension

Easier

- Use a large ball.
- Stand closer to the net/on the mat.

Harder

- Play on a larger court.
- Use a higher net.
- Move the mats further from the net.

Extension

- Increase the numbers of players.
- Explore tennis principles.

Full Activity Description

The aim of the game is to score points by throwing a ball into the opponent's court area and making it bounce twice.

Play the game 1 v 1. Use a low net (bench to short tennis height) on a court that is relatively long and narrow. Put a gym mat on either side of the net, about 1m away from the net, and make the court a little larger than this. Use throwing and catching skills.

Once the children can play the game confidently, move on to introduce hitting the ball with a racket after it has bounced. A partner playing with the hitter should feed the ball. Try adapting the rules so the partner has to catch the ball before feeding it to be hit. More able players will be able to rally without a partner feeding the ball. They may need more than 1 bounce.

This game is easiest with a big ball that bounces well. It can also be played by pushing or sliding the ball across a line that is being defended. (This is easier for some children who have difficulties with coordination.)

CATCH THE BALL BEFORE IT LANDS ON THE TARGET

Activity 4, Upper Key Stage 1/Lower to Middle Key Stage 2 (Age 7–9)

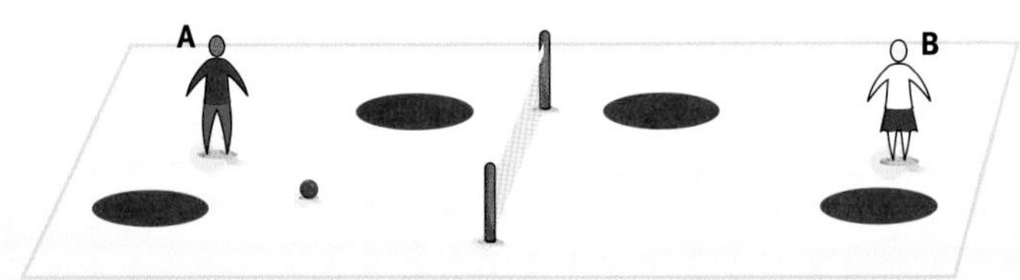

1 Person **A:** Throw **short** and **low** to the **nearest** target.

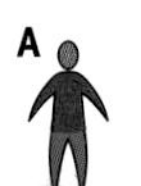

2 Person **A:** Throw **long** and **high** to the furthest target.

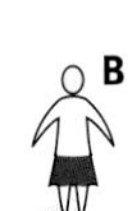

3 Person **B:** Catch the ball before it bounces.

LEADER NOTES

Objectives

Pupils should:

- be able to catch the ball before it lands on the target
- know and understand that throws should be different depending on where you want the ball to land
- continue to develop fundamental movement skills and become increasingly competent and confident
- apply and develop a broader range of skills, learning how to use them in different ways
- be able to engage in competitive and cooperative physical activities in a range of increasingly challenging situations, and enjoy communicating, collaborating and competing with each other
- start to develop an understanding of how to improve, and learn how to evaluate and recognise their own success.

Differentiation and Extension

Easier

- Remove a target.
- Make targets larger.

Harder

- Place targets closer together.
- Make areas the defender is not allowed to stand in.

Extension

- Use badminton equipment.
- Use larger teams with their own defined areas.

Full Activity Description

The aim of the game is to score points by getting a small soft ball or beanbag to land in 1 of 2 targets.

Play the game 1 v 1. Use a high net on a long narrow court (about 3–5m long on each side of the net and 1–2m wide). Position a target near the front of the court on either side of the net, and another towards the back of the court. Encourage the children to use short, low throws to try to hit the target at the front, and long, high throws to try to hit the target at the back. Their opponent's aim is to intercept the ball or beanbag before it bounces.

Later, a racket can be used to hit a ball or shuttlecock. The same technique of partner feeding can be used as in Activity 3, but the feed should be a full toss.

CATCH THE BALL BEFORE IT LANDS ON THE TARGET

Activity 5, Upper Key Stage 1/Lower to Middle Key Stage 2 (Age 7–9)

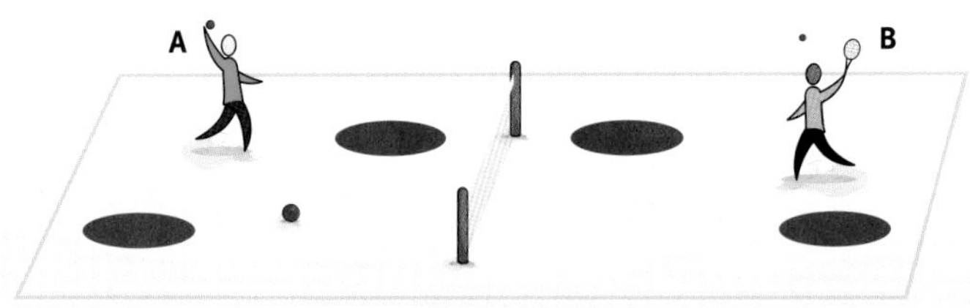

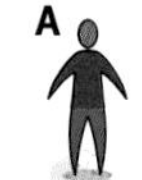

1 Person **A:** Throw **short** and **low** to the **nearest** target.

2 Person **A:** Throw **long** and **high** to the furthest target.

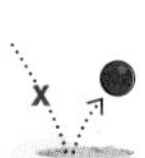

3 Person **B:** Hit the ball before it bounces.

LEADER NOTES

Objectives

Pupils should:

- be able to aim in the direction of a target
- know and understand the difference between throwing 'short and low' and 'long and high'
- continue to develop fundamental movement skills and become increasingly competent and confident
- apply and develop a broader range of skills, learning how to use them in different ways
- be able to engage in competitive and cooperative physical activities in a range of increasingly challenging situations, and enjoy communicating, collaborating and competing with each other
- start to develop an understanding of how to improve, and learn how to evaluate and recognise their own success.

Differentiation and Extension

Easier

- Remove a target.
- Make targets larger.

Harder

- Place targets closer together.
- Make areas the defender is not allowed to stand in.

Extension

- Use badminton equipment.
- Use larger teams with their own defined areas.

Full Activity Description

The aim of the game is to score points by getting a small soft ball or beanbag to land in 1 of 2 targets.

Play the game 1 v 1. Use a high net on a long, narrow court (about 3–5m long on each side of the net, and 1–2m wide). Position a target near the front of the court on either side of the net, and another towards the back of the court. Encourage the children to use short, low throws to try to hit the target at the front, and long, high throws to try to hit the target at the back. Their opponent's aim is to intercept the ball or beanbag before it bounces.

Later, a racket can be used to hit a ball or shuttlecock. The same technique of partner feeding can be used as in Activity 3, but the feed should be a full toss.

THINK OF YOUR OWN GAME

Activity 6, Upper Key Stage 1/Lower to Middle Key Stage 2 (Age 7–9)

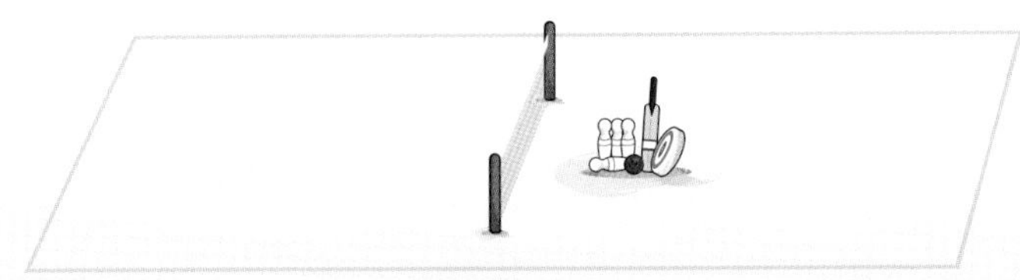

1 Choose a new game to teach to friends.

2 Choose a good scoring **system** for your game.

3 Decide what you would **change** in your game.

>>> LEADER NOTES

Objectives

Pupils should:

- be able to teach friends their new game
- know and understand how to score points in their new game
- continue to develop fundamental movement skills and become increasingly competent and confident
- apply and develop a broader range of skills, learning how to use them in different ways
- be able to engage in competitive and cooperative physical activities in a range of increasingly challenging situations, and enjoy communicating, collaborating and competing with each other
- start to develop an understanding of how to improve, and learn how to evaluate and recognise their own success.

Differentiation and Extension

Easier

- Ask leading questions such as ‘Which part of the game would you like to change/do you not like?’
- Place all available equipment on show.

Harder

- Place pupils in randomly assigned groups.

Extension

- Teach the game to other groups/rest of the class.

Full Activity Description

Ask the children to adapt the rules, equipment or skills of the game they are playing so it suits them better. Then ask them to make up a new net game, with a good scoring system. They should be able to play their game well and teach it to others in the class.

HIT THE BALL BACK BEFORE IT BOUNCES TWICE

Activity 7, Middle to Upper Key Stage 2 (Age 9–11)

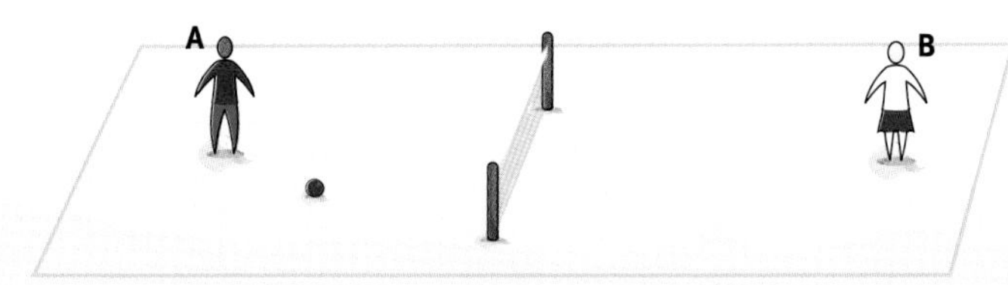

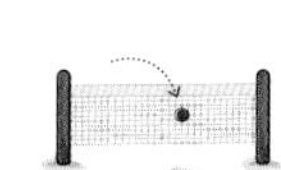

1 Choose how to send the ball over the net.

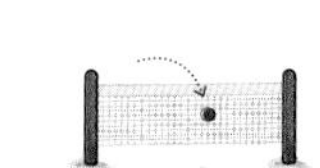

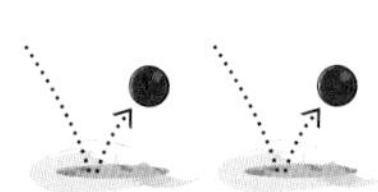

2 Hit the ball over the net **before** it bounces twice.

Continue if the ball lands **over** the line.

>>> LEADER NOTES

Objectives

Pupils should:

- be able to anticipate the travel path of a ball
- know and understand where best to stand in preparation for receiving a ball
- continue to apply and develop a broader range of skills, learning how to use them in different ways
- enjoy communicating, collaborating and competing with each other
- develop an understanding of how to improve in different physical activities and sports, and learn how to evaluate and recognise their own success.

Differentiation and Extension

Easier

- Play without a net.
- Play with a partner.

Harder

- Play with a higher net.
- Play with partners who work in designated sides only.

Extension

- Play on a wide, short court.

Full Activity Description

The aim of the game is to score points by hitting a ball into your opponent's court and the ball bouncing twice.

Play the game 1 v 1 on a long, narrow court that is about half the size of a short-tennis or badminton court. Use a racket and suitable ball. Players score a point when the ball lands in the court and bounces twice. Ask the children to choose their own way to start and restart the game. If the ball lands outside the court, the rally continues – no points are lost for hitting the ball out or into the net. The game can also be played on a wide, short court.

HIT THE BALL BACK BEFORE IT BOUNCES TWICE

Activity 8, Middle to Upper Key Stage 2 (Age 9–11)

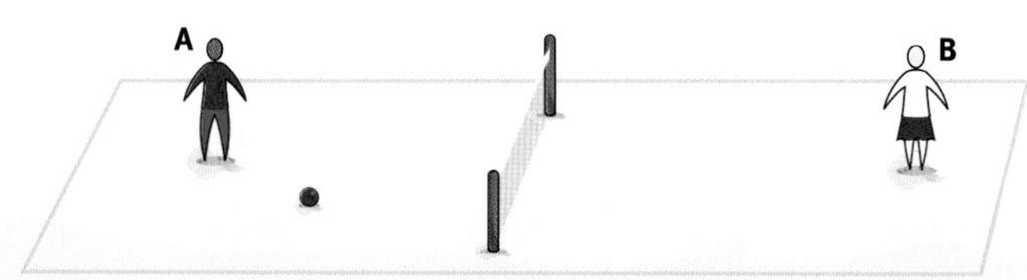

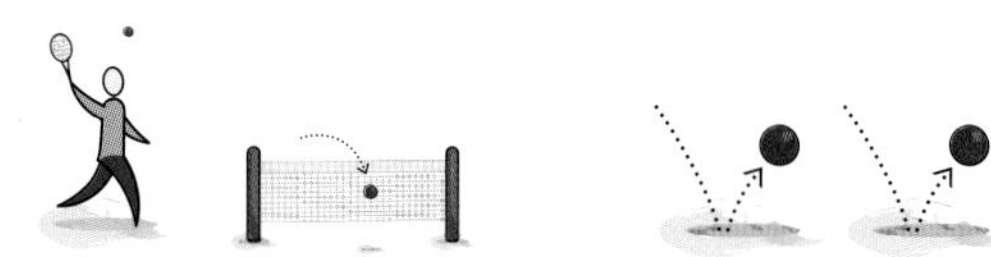

1 Hit the ball over the net **before** it bounces twice.

2 **Continue** if the ball lands **outside** the court.

3 Score a point if the ball lands **inside** the court.

>>> LEADER NOTES

Objectives

Pupils should:

- be able to move quickly and easily around a narrow playing area
- know and understand that it is advantageous to keep the ball inside the playing area
- continue to apply and develop a broader range of skills, learning how to use them in different ways
- enjoy communicating, collaborating and competing with each other
- develop an understanding of how to improve in different physical activities and sports, and learn how to evaluate and recognise their own success.

Differentiation and Extension

Easier

- Lower the net.
- Play with a shuttlecock.

Harder

- Make the court narrower and longer.
- Hit the ball against the wall in half of the space.

Extension

- Explore the badminton points system.
- Use volleyball skills: throwing and catching/catching and pushing.

Full Activity Description

This game is played in the same way as Activity 7 with the following changes:

- Raise the height of the net so it is above players' head height.
- Make the court a little narrower and longer.
- Introduce the rule that a point is scored by the hitter if the ball lands in court (this teaches the children basic volleying).

It may be helpful to play with a shuttlecock, rather than a ball.

PLAY TENNIS INDOORS WITH A LOW NET

Activity 9, Middle to Upper Key Stage 2 (Age 9–11)

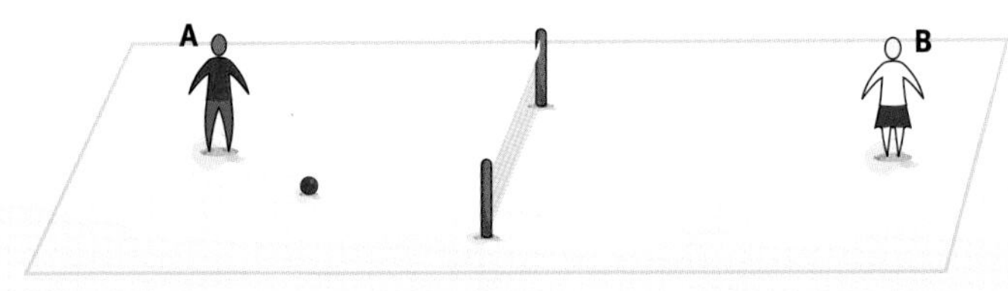

1 Hit the ball over the net **after** 1 bounce.

2 Score a point if the ball is **not** returned after 1 bounce.

3 Only score if you served the ball.

>>> LEADER NOTES

Objectives

Pupils should:

- be able to use a basic tennis scoring system
- know and understand a basic tennis scoring system
- continue to apply and develop a broader range of skills, learning how to use them in different ways
- enjoy communicating, collaborating and competing with each other
- develop an understanding of how to improve in different physical activities and sports, and learn how to evaluate and recognise their own success.

Differentiation and Extension

Easier

- Remove the net.
- Play without a racket or ball.

Harder

- Make the net higher.
- Play using court service areas.

Extension

- Play a tournament or 'round robin'.

Full Activity Description

Play short-tennis doubles and singles using the basic rules on a full court.

PLAY TENNIS INDOORS WITH A LOW NET

Activity 10, Upper Key Stage 2/Key Stage 3 (Age 10–14)

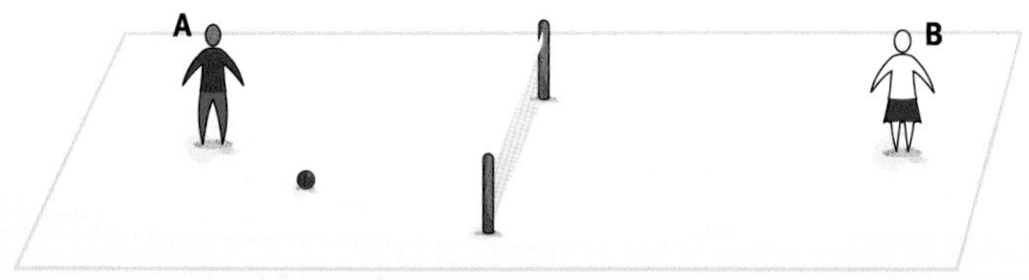

1 Agree with your partner how you will send the ball at the start.

2 Agree on a scoring system.

3 Score extra points if your partner lets the ball bounce twice.

››› LEADER NOTES

Objectives

Pupils should:

- be able to describe their scoring system
- know and understand that the ball should only bounce once on the court
- continue to implement and develop a broader range of skills, learning how to use them in different ways
- enjoy communicating, collaborating and competing with each other
- develop an understanding of how to succeed in different activities and sports, and learn how to evaluate and recognise their own success
- understand what makes a performance effective and apply these principles to their own and others' work
- become more competent, confident and expert in their techniques, and apply them across different sports and activities
- develop the confidence and interest to get involved in exercise, sports and activities outside school.

Differentiation and Extension

Easier

- Make the court smaller.
- Use a slower ball.
- Allow the ball to bounce more than once.

Harder

- Use a faster, higher-bouncing ball.
- Vary the width and length of the court.
- Use volleying only.

Extension

- Play doubles games.
- Use target areas for additional point scoring within a game.

Full Activity Description

The purpose of the game for pupils is to score more points than their opponent by getting the ball to bounce once in their opponent's court and then a second time. Play 1 v 1 on a modified court 3–5m² on each side of a low net. Use a suitable racket and ball. Players should agree rules on how to start the game, restart the game after a point is won, finish the game, and on a scoring system. The chosen game should reflect known games (eg tennis, badminton or volleyball).

SCORE POINTS BY MAKING THE BALL LAND ON THE OPPOSITE SIDE OF THE COURT

Activity 11, Upper Key Stage 2/Key Stage 3 (Age 10–14)

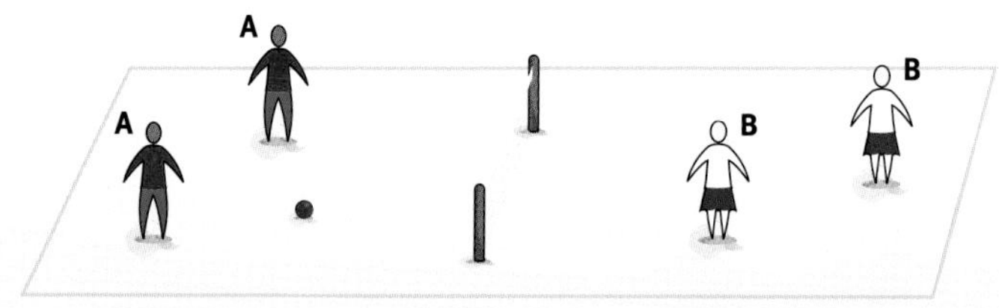

1 Agree with your partner at the start on how you will send the ball.

2 Agree on a scoring system.

3 Score extra points if your opponents let the ball bounce twice.

>>> LEADER NOTES

Objectives

Pupils should:

- be able to play as part of a pair
- know and understand that the aim is to hit the ball so it lands in the opponents' half of the court
- continue to implement and develop a broader range of skills, learning how to use them in different ways
- enjoy communicating, collaborating and competing with each other
- develop an understanding of how to succeed in different activities and sports, and learn how to evaluate and recognise their own success
- understand what makes a performance effective and apply these principles to their own and others' work
- become more competent, confident and expert in their techniques, and apply them across different sports and activities
- develop the confidence and interest to get involved in exercise, sports and activities outside school.

Differentiation and Extension

Easier

- Play singles on a narrower court.
- Allow players to catch the ball before returning it.

Harder

- Use a faster, higher-bouncing ball.
- Make the court larger.

Extension

- Use rackets and shuttlecocks.
- Use target areas for additional point scoring within a game.

Full Activity Description

The purpose is to score points by getting the ball to land in the opponents' court. Play 2 v 2 over a net that is above head height on a court that is about 5m x 5m on each side of the net.

OUTDOOR AND ADVENTURE

››› FOLLOW THE ARROWS TO FIND THE SHAPES

Activity 1, Early Key Stage 1 (Age 5–6)

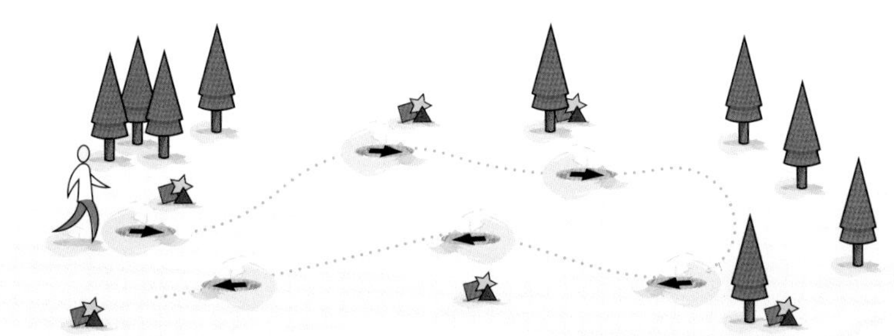

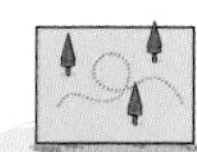

1 Walk around your trail, following the arrows.

2 Walk to **each** arrow and **look** for a shape.

3 When you find a shape, **tick** it on your sheet.

»» LEADER NOTES

Objectives

Pupils should:

- be able to follow a trail of arrows
- know and understand the word 'trail'
- develop fundamental movement skills
- be able to engage in competitive and cooperative activities in a range of increasingly challenging situations.

Differentiation and Extension

Easier

- Follow the trail in a pair/small group/with a leader.
- Follow a shorter trail.
- Find 1–2 shapes at a time and have them checked before continuing.

Harder

- Add a time limit to find all the shapes.
- Follow a longer trail individually.
- Develop the tick sheet, matching pictures to writing or clues to a puzzle.

Extension

- Follow a trail in the school grounds or local green area.
- Link clues to the location of the next arrow and clue (like a treasure hunt).

Full Activity Description

See if you can follow a trail marked by arrows or a long piece of string that goes round the classroom or hall. When you find an object, picture or shape on the trail, match it up to the pictures on your check sheet.

RESCUE THE OBJECTS FROM THE RIVER

Activity 2, Middle/Upper Key Stage 1 (Age 6–7)

1 Use the equipment to **rescue** the objects.

2 **Do not** put your hands or body in the river.

3 Work as a team to **empty** the river.

››› LEADER NOTES

Objectives

Pupils should:

- be able to work as part of team to complete an activity
- know and understand how equipment can be used in different ways to perform an activity
- develop fundamental movement skills, becoming increasingly competent and confident
- access a broad range of opportunities to extend their agility, balance and coordination, individually and with others
- be able to engage in competitive and cooperative physical activities in a range of increasingly challenging situations.

Differentiation and Extension

Easier

- Give lives/chances for when a body part 'touches the river'.
- Place the river items closer to the pupils.
- Allow a practice/experiment time.

Harder

- Set a time limit for 'rescuing' the items.
- Give items scores depending on the difficulty of retrieval.
- Complete the activity in silence.

Extension

- 'Fish' items out of a bucket ('pond').
- Add levels and shapes to the river.

Full Activity Description

See how many things you can rescue from the 'river' without putting any part of your body, including your hands, into the river area. The river is marked by 2 lines (rope or benches). You can only use the equipment you find on the riverbank to help you (eg skipping ropes, plastic hockey sticks and small bats). Work as a team to get everything out.

>>> FIND THE CONTROL POINT

Activity 3, Upper Key Stage 1/Lower to Middle Key Stage 2 (Age 7–9)

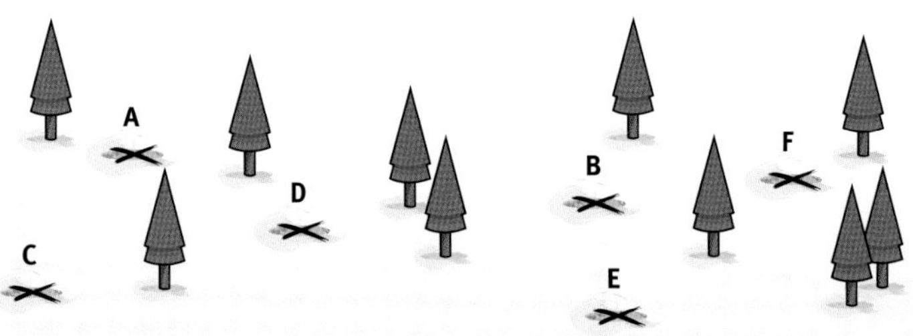

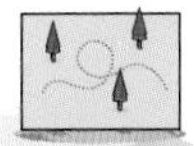

A, B, C ...

1 Use a map to find **3** control points.

2 Return to your base.

A, B, C ...

3 **Find** the other control points.

››› LEADER NOTES

Objectives

Pupils should:

- be able to follow a map to find a control point
- know and understand the terms 'control point' and 'orienteering'
- become increasingly competent in a range of skills, and access a broad range of activities
- apply and develop these skills, learning how to use them in different ways
- enjoy communicating, collaborating, and competing and cooperating in physical activities in a range of increasingly challenging situations
- start to develop an understanding of how to improve in different activities, and learn how to evaluate and recognise their own success.

Differentiation and Extension

Easier

- Complete a trail inside the school.
- Follow photo trails or easily recognisable features (eg 'toilet' and 'fire exit' signs).
- Work in pairs and/or small groups.

Harder

- Use a map with simple grid references or numbered boxes.
- Work against a time limit.
- Work independently and/or as part of a race to complete the course.

Extension

- Remove a control point and task pupils to find out which is missing.
- Complete in teams, finding the control points in specific orders.
- Repeat the activity in an unfamiliar area.

Full Activity Description

Use a simple map of the playground or school fields to complete a course with 8–12 controls. Check 3–4 controls and then return to base before finding the next ones.

>>> LEAD YOUR BLINDFOLDED PARTNER

Activity 4, Upper Key Stage 1/Lower to Middle Key Stage 2 (Age 7–9)

1 Tie a blindfold on your partner.

2 Lead them using your voice or fingertips.

3 **Repeat** using your own communication signals.

>>> LEADER NOTES

Objectives

Pupils should:

- be able to devise different methods of communication
- know and understand how to deliver clear and non-confusing instructions
- become increasingly competent in a range of skills, and access a broad range of activities
- apply and develop these skills, learning how to use them in different ways
- enjoy communicating, collaborating, and competing and cooperating in physical activities in a range of increasingly challenging situations
- start to develop an understanding of how to improve in different activities, and learn how to evaluate and recognise their own success.

Differentiation and Extension

Easier

- Allow the blindfolded person to place 1 hand on the leader's shoulders.
- Walk the route without blindfolds first.

Harder

- Add obstacles within the safe area.
- Add numbers of other pairs within the same safe area.

Extension

- Make a route on difficult terrain.
- Use ropes for the 'blind' to hold and follow, using the leader to instruct them through obstacles.

Full Activity Description

Carry out this activity with a partner. 1 of you put on a blindfold. The person without the blindfold should then lead their partner around a safe area given by the teacher. You can only use voice and fingertip contact to lead your partner (without pushing or pulling). When you have both had a go, repeat the activity without using your voice, and using your own signal system.

>>> CROSS THE RIVER BY MAKING A BRIDGE

Activity 5, Upper Key Stage 1/Lower to Middle Key Stage 2 (Age 7–9)

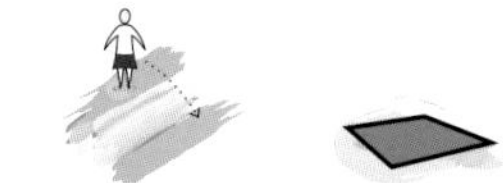

1 Cross the river on mats.

2 Cross the river by stepping into hoops.

3 Cross the river using cones or discs.

››› LEADER NOTES

Objectives

Pupils should:

- be able to decide how to choose and use equipment to best solve a challenge
- know and understand how to communicate ideas within a team so a challenge is completed
- become increasingly competent in a range of skills, and access a broad range of activities
- apply and develop these skills, learning how to use them in different ways
- enjoy communicating, collaborating, and competing and cooperating in physical activities in a range of increasingly challenging situations
- start to develop an understanding of how to improve in different activities, and learn how to evaluate and recognise their own success.

Differentiation and Extension

Easier

- Work in pairs or small groups.
- Give lives/chances for when a body part touches the river.

Harder

- Set the river on uneven/rough terrain.
- Set a time limit to complete each challenge in.

Extension

- Groups devise challenges for others to solve.

Full Activity Description

Take part in some adventure games (eg cross a barrier or space using a floating bridge – 2 large, easily moved objects such as hoops or mats; cross a swamp using small cones or discs as stepping stones).

FIND THE CONTROL POINTS WITHIN THE TIME LIMIT

Activity 6, Middle to Upper Key Stage 2 (Age 9–11)

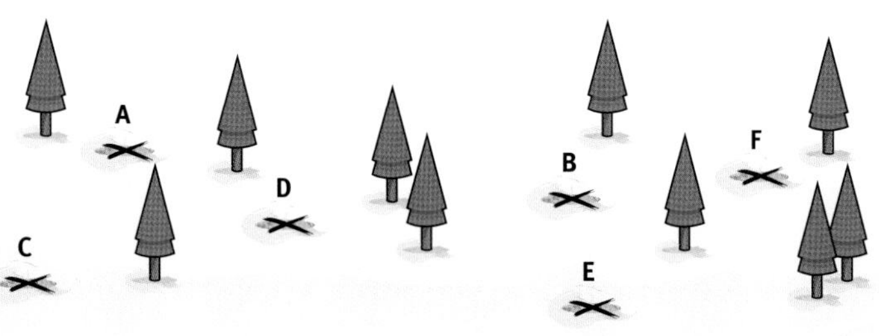

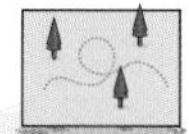

1 Use a map to find the control points.

2 Find the control points in less than **45** minutes.

3 Work in a pair or small group.

>>> LEADER NOTES

Objectives

Pupils should:

- be able to set and follow a pace to complete a physical challenge within a time limit
- know and understand how to 'orient' a map to show their direction of travel
- continue to apply and develop a broader range of skills, learning how to use them in different ways
- enjoy communicating, collaborating and competing with each other
- develop an understanding of how to improve in different physical activities and sports, and learn how to evaluate and recognise their own success.

Differentiation and Extension

Easier

- Use a pair relay system where a pair finds 1 control and returns to base.
- Follow photo trails or easily recognisable features or signs.
- Work in a familiar area.

Harder

- Use a map with grid references or numbered boxes.
- Work against a time limit.
- Work independently and/or as part of a race to complete the course.

Extension

- Set up problem-solving activities at each control point.
- Have the groups devise a route and draw a map for others to follow.

Full Activity Description

Working in pairs or small groups, complete an orienteering course using a map. Your challenge is to find 8–12 controls in less than 45 minutes. The course will be in your school grounds or a local park you know.

>>> LEAD YOUR BLINDFOLDED PEOPLE

Activity 7, Middle to Upper Key Stage 2 (Age 9–11)

1 Lead your blindfolded partner on **rough terrain.**

2 Direct a blindfolded group to a **new place.**

3 Direct a blindfolded group along a rope maze

in the woods.

LEADER NOTES

Objectives

Pupils should:

- be able to direct single and groups of blindfolded people around areas and obstacles without physical contact
- know and understand what a 'rope maze' is, and how to make and lead someone around it
- continue to apply and develop a broader range of skills, learning how to use them in different ways
- enjoy communicating, collaborating and competing with each other
- develop an understanding of how to improve in different physical activities and sports, and learn how to evaluate and recognise their own success.

Differentiation and Extension

Easier

- Let the leader have a 'helper'.
- Lead the groups in a familiar and enclosed area.

Harder

- Specify 1 way they must use to communicate.
- Lead the groups in areas of rough terrain.

Extension

- Plant a 'cheat' in the group who purposely goes the wrong way at times.
- Introduce a play on words (eg doing the opposite of every verbal instruction).

Full Activity Description

Take part in a range of activities that involve working with, and trusting, others in your class. Your teacher will suggest activities, such as:

- a person who can see leading their blindfolded partner over difficult ground (this might include obstacles), or helping their partner carry out some simple activities
- a person who can see, but is not allowed to move, helping a group of blindfolded people complete an activity (eg making a square from a line or rope)
- a blindfolded group following a 'night line' – a line or rope around, over or through a safe course.

TAKE THE TREASURE CHEST OVER THE ELECTRIC FENCE

Activity 8, Middle to Upper Key Stage 2 (Age 9–11)

1 All of your group cross over the electric fence.

2 Take the treasure, but do not touch the fence!

3 Only use equipment your group is given.

››› LEADER NOTES

Objectives

Pupils should:

- be able to solve a problem as part of a team
- know and understand how the same principles can be adapted to solve similar challenges
- continue to apply and develop a broader range of skills, learning how to use them in different ways
- enjoy communicating, collaborating and competing with each other
- develop an understanding of how to improve in different physical activities and sports, and learn how to evaluate and recognise their own success.

Differentiation and Extension

Easier

- Give lives/chances for when a body part touches the fence.
- Use a smaller space and lower fence.
- Allow more time to complete the activity, prompt possible answers.

Harder

- Use larger groups.
- Set a time limit for completion.
- Give more equipment to carry.

Extension

- Groups devise challenges for others and/or themselves to solve.
- Repeat the challenge with levels and less equipment to assist.

Full Activity Description

In teams, complete a range of problem-solving adventure games (eg cross an 'electric fence' made from elastic without any of the team or the equipment you are carrying touching it; cross a divide using stepping stones while carrying 'precious' materials).

PLAN TO COMPLETE AND COMPLETE AN ORIENTEERING COURSE

Activity 9, Upper Key Stage 2/Key Stage 3 (Age 10–14)

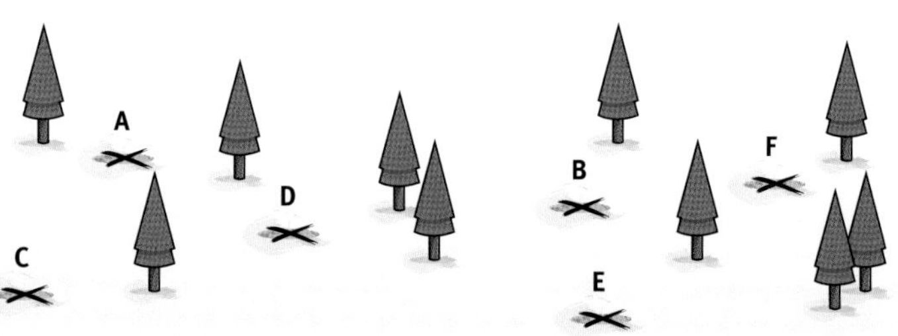

1 On your own, find all of the controls.

2 Spend 10 minutes planning how you will complete the course. Hand in your plan.

3 Record the order and the time you arrive at each control.

»» LEADER NOTES

Objectives

Pupils should:

- be able to develop a preferred order of finding control points based on efficiency and difficulty
- know and understand how to assess the efficiency and difficulty of travelling to each control point
- build on, and embed, the skills they have already learnt, and become more competent, confident and expert in their techniques
- apply these skills and techniques across a range of activities
- understand what makes a performance effective and how to apply these principles to their own and others' work
- start to develop confidence and interest to get involved in activities outside school.

Differentiation and Extension

Easier

- Use a pair relay system where a pair finds 1 control and returns to base.
- Plan shorter trails.
- Work in a familiar area.

Harder

- Use a map with grid references.
- Work against a time limit.
- Use compasses and bearings to complete the course.

Extension

- Set up problem-solving activities at each control point.
- Have the groups devise a route and draw a map for others to follow.
- Change directions to clues.

Full Activity Description

Pupils complete a solo orienteering course with 6–12 controls set in familiar terrain (eg the school site or local parkland). They spend 10 minutes planning how they will complete the course, then hand in a copy of the plan before departure. They record the order in which they visit the controls and the time taken to move between them.

>>> COMPLETE THE ORIENTEERING ACTIVITIES WHILE CARRYING A MYSTERY OBJECT

Activity 10, Upper Key Stage 2/Key Stage 3 (Age 10–14)

1 Work in a group of 4–5 competing against other teams.

2 Carry a 40kg pack between your team through all the controls.

3 Complete the activity at each control and collect a 'key' from the last control.

>>> LEADER NOTES

Objectives

Pupils should:

- be able to delegate roles within the team depending on individuals' strengths and weaknesses
- know and understand the importance of sharing tasks throughout a physically demanding activity
- build on, and embed, the skills they have already learnt, and become more competent, confident and expert in their techniques
- apply these skills and techniques across a range of activities
- understand what makes a performance effective and how to apply these principles to their own and others' work
- start to develop confidence and interest to get involved in activities outside school.

Differentiation and Extension

Easier

- Use a pair relay system where a pair finds 1 control and returns to base.
- Use smaller slopes, 'river' crossing lengths and decreased wall heights.
- Award points for explaining how they would like to complete the activity.

Harder

- Add constraints between activities (eg walking blindfolded).
- Limit practice time and/or work against a time limit.
- Add individual constraints (eg no one to carry the weight twice).

Extension

- Expand each activity and focus on methods for completing each one.
- Assign groups the activity of instructing others on how to complete set activities.

Full Activity Description

Pupils can work in a small group of 4–5 to solve a series of problems based around a circuit of activities. Each group will compete against other teams. They will carry an awkward load, such as a pack of supplies weighing approximately 40kg. The pack should not get wet or touch the ground. They will have to carry the object through a difficult maze, over a height of at least 2m, across a stream or a series of obstacles, up and down difficult slopes and, finally, retrieve a 'key' from a difficult position.

›››

SWIMMING

MOVE AROUND THE POOL

Activity 1, Pre-curriculum/Early Key Stage 1 (Age 4–5)

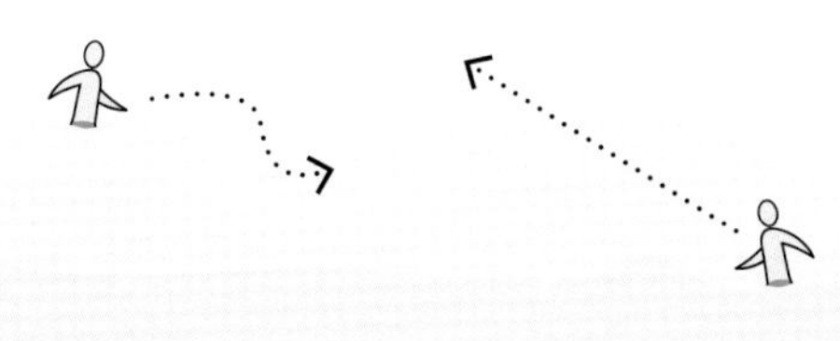

1 Move **around** or **across** the pool.

2 Try hopping, jumping, running and floating.

3 How fast and how **quietly** can you move?

LEADER NOTES

Objectives

Pupils should:

- be able to attempt to hop, skip, jump and float in a swimming pool
- know and understand what swimming aids are and how they should be worn
- develop fundamental movement skills, becoming increasingly competent and confident
- access a broad range of opportunities to extend their agility, balance and coordination.

Differentiation and Extension

Easier

- Hold on to the wall while walking.
- Use adult/leader support.

Harder

- Go backwards and sideways.
- Go into a deeper area.

Extension

- Play 'follow my leader'.
- Participate in individual and/or team relay races.

Full Activity Description

Individually, in pairs or small groups, move around or across the pool while wearing swimming aids. See how fast or quietly you can move across the pool, using walking, running, jumping, hopping, skipping, lunging and floating, and swimming actions.

HOW LONG CAN YOU KEEP YOUR FEET OFF THE FLOOR?

Activity 2, Early Key Stage 1 (Age 5–6)

1 Make body shapes: tuck and stretch.

2 Lie on your front and your back.

3 Hold your breath.

LEADER NOTES

Objectives

Pupils should:

- be able to take their feet off the pool floor
- know and understand that it is still safe when their feet are off the pool floor
- develop fundamental movement skills, becoming increasingly competent and confident
- access a broad range of opportunities to extend their agility, balance and coordination
- engage in competitive (both against self and others) activities in a range of increasingly challenging situations.

Differentiation and Extension

Easier

- Hold on to the wall while taking feet off the floor.
- Use adult/leader support.
- Use swimming aids that give more support.

Harder

- Use fewer/no swimming aids.
- Put faces/heads in the water.
- Plunge under the surface.

Extension

- Participate in timed competitions.
- Play 'Simon says'.

Full Activity Description

How long can you stay still with your feet off the ground when:

- using different body shapes (eg tuck and stretch)
- lying on your front or back
- holding your breath?

SWIM AS FAR AS YOU CAN

Activity 3, Middle to Upper Key Stage 1 (Age 6–7)

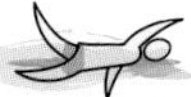

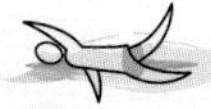

1 Try to swim **5** metres.

2 Try to swim **25** metres.

3 You can use armbands and floats.

>>> LEADER NOTES

Objectives

Pupils should:

- be able to attempt to swim 25m – 1 length of a standard pool
- know and understand the distances of a width (10m) and length (25m)
- continue to develop fundamental movement skills, becoming increasingly competent and confident
- engage in competitive (both against self and others) activities in a range of increasingly challenging situations.

Differentiation and Extension

Easier

- Swim next to the wall.
- Use adult/leader support.
- Put floating markers in the water to reach for.

Harder

- Swim without aids.
- Swim down the middle of the pool.
- Try to swim on their front and back.

Extension

- Undertake distance challenges.
- Participate in individual and/or team relay races.

Full Activity Description

See how far you can swim. Try to cover 5–20 metres using swimming aids (eg armbands and floats).

SWIM AS FAST AS YOU CAN

Activity 4, Lower to Middle Key Stage 2 (Age 8–9)

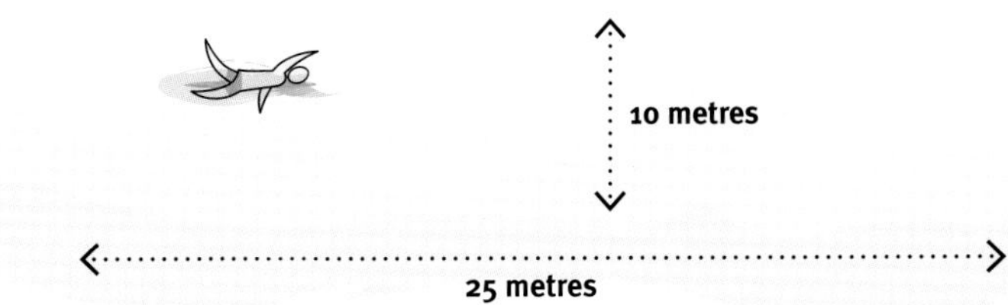

1 Swim **10** metres as fast as you can.

2 Swim **25** metres as fast as you can.

3 Swim **50** metres as fast as you can.

>>> LEADER NOTES

Objectives

Pupils should:

- be able to attempt to swim at a fast pace
- know and understand differences in strokes when swum fast compared to when swum slowly
- continue to implement and develop a broader range of skills, learning how to use them and implement them in different ways
- enjoy competing
- develop an understanding of how to succeed, and learn how to evaluate and recognise their own success.

Differentiation and Extension

Easier

- Swim next to the wall.
- Use adult/leader support aids.
- Put floating markers in the water to reach for.

Harder

- Swim without aids.
- Swim down the middle of the pool.
- Try swimming on their front and back.

Extension

- Count the number of strokes used to cover the distance.
- Swim using a given number of breaths.
- Use set rules for each stroke.

Full Activity Description

How fast can you swim:

- 10 metres
- 25 metres
- 50 metres?

SWIM FAST WITH A TEAM

Activity 5, Middle to Upper Key Stage 2 (Age 9–11)

1 Time your team sprinting **100, 200** and **400** metres.

2 Do not put your feet on the floor.

3 Everyone must swim, 1 swimmer at a time.

LEADER NOTES

Objectives

Pupils should:

- be able to use multiples of 25 to work out length distances
- know and understand that some strokes are naturally faster and easier than others
- continue to implement and develop a broader range of skills, learning how to use them and implement them in different ways
- enjoy communicating, collaborating and competing with each other
- develop an understanding of how to succeed, and learn how to evaluate and recognise their own success.

Differentiation and Extension

Easier

- Allow a weaker swimmer to complete less distance.
- Use swimming aids.

Harder

- Swim with at least 2 strokes.
- Swim with the team using the same or 2 different strokes only.

Extension

- Swim as a team for a set time period, measuring the distance travelled.
- Add objects to the path of travel/incorporate an obstacle course.

Full Activity Description

How fast can you swim:

- 10 metres
- 25 metres
- 50 metres?

Only 1 person can swim at a time, and everyone must swim part of the distance. No feet may touch the ground. Try the challenge 4–5 times over several lessons and try to get your team to swim the distance faster.

SWIM A PERSONAL SURVIVAL CIRCUIT

Activity 6, Middle to Upper Key Stage 2 (Age 9–11)

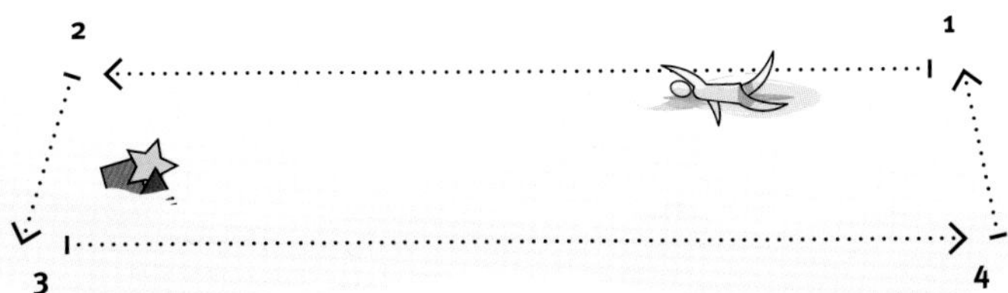

Swim around a circuit for an agreed time or distance:

1 Do not put your feet on the floor.

2 Swim on and under the water.

3 **Float, carry** and **fetch** objects from the floor.

LEADER NOTES

Objectives

Pupils should:

- be able to attempt to collect objects from the pool floor
- know and understand the term 'circuit'
- continue to implement and develop a broader range of skills, learning how to use them and implement them in different ways
- enjoy competing
- develop an understanding of how to succeed in different physical activities, and learn how to evaluate and recognise their own success.

Differentiation and Extension

Easier

- Set a shorter time or distance.
- Use swimming aids.

Harder

- Tackle more obstacles on the circuit.
- Increase the speed of performance.

Extension

- Perform relay races.

Full Activity Description

How long can you keep going around a personal survival obstacle course without touching the ground? Try to keep going for set lengths of time (eg 5 minutes, 8 minutes, 12 minutes). The course should involve:

- swimming on the surface
- swimming underwater
- carrying equipment
- floating or sculling for a set period of time
- retrieving equipment from the bottom of the pool.

>>> PRACTISE STARTS AND TURNS

Activity 7, Upper Key Stage 2/Key Stage 3 (Age 10–14)

1 Time how long it takes you to swim 2 lengths.

2 Try different starts and turns to try to get a faster time.

3 Try swimming the same and different strokes to see if you get a faster time.

LEADER NOTES

Objectives

Pupils should:

- be able to attempt a form of start and turn for each stroke
- know and understand the official starts and turns for each stroke
- continue to implement and develop a broader range of skills, learning how to use them in different ways
- develop an understanding of how to succeed in different activities and sports, and learn how to evaluate and recognise their own success
- become more competent, confident and expert in their techniques.

Differentiation and Extension

Easier

- Swim widths instead of lengths.
- Swim next to the wall.
- Use swimming aids.

Harder

- Set specific strokes and starts to be used.
- Set specific time targets.
- Increase the distance.

Extension

- Perform relay races.
- Compare width and length times for the same distance.

Full Activity Description

Ask pupils to try different starts and turns to investigate the effect on the time it takes them to swim 2 lengths. Encourage them to see if there is a difference when they use a particular stroke, a different stroke or a combination of both strokes. Choose their 2 best strokes to work on. Work on improving times.

SWIM DISTANCES AS A TEAM

Activity 8, Upper Key Stage 2/Key Stage 3 (Age 10–14)

1 Using 3 different strokes, swim 200m and 400m as a team.

2 Share the distances and strokes fairly.

3 Try different ways to improve the speed and efficiency of the strokes.

LEADER NOTES

Objectives

Pupils should:

- be able to contribute to the evaluation of strokes and swimming performance
- know and understand the phrase 'efficiency of strokes'
- continue to implement and develop a broader range of skills, learning how to use them in different ways
- enjoy communicating, collaborating and competing with each other
- develop an understanding of how to succeed in different activities and sports, and learn how to evaluate and recognise their own success
- become more competent, confident and expert in their techniques.

Differentiation and Extension

Easier

- Swim widths instead of lengths/decrease the overall distance.
- Swim next to the wall/use swimming aids.
- Use only 1–2 strokes.

Harder

- Decrease group size.
- Set specific time targets.
- Increase the distance.

Extension

- Perform relay races.
- Compare the use of 1, 2, 3 and 4 strokes.

Full Activity Description

Investigate the most effective way of swimming distances between 200m and 400m as a group/relay team using 3 different strokes. Share out the distance and strokes fairly. Explore ways of improving speed and efficiency.

COMPLETE A PERSONAL SURVIVAL CHALLENGE

Activity 9, Upper Key Stage 2/Key Stage 3 (Age 10–14)

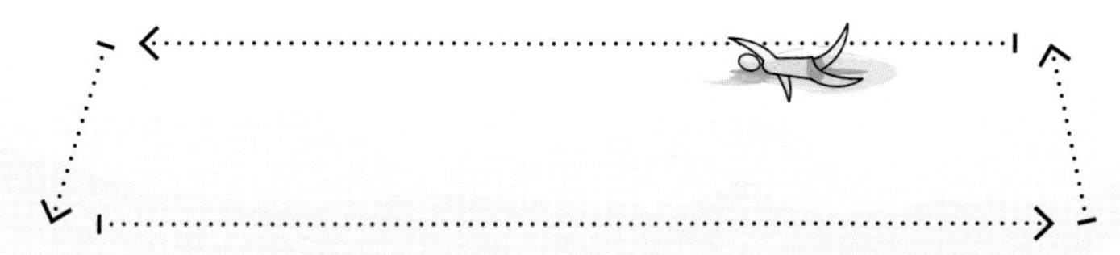

1 Make a personal survival challenge that lasts 6–10 minutes.

2 Include swimming, surface diving, floating, sculling and getting into/out of the water.

3 Find ways to improve efficiency and safety.

LEADER NOTES

Objectives

Pupils should:

- be able to complete a survival challenge of 5 activities in the water
- know and understand the terms 'surface diving' and 'sculling'
- continue to implement and develop a broader range of skills, learning how to use them in different ways
- develop an understanding of how to succeed in different activities and sports, and learn how to evaluate and recognise their own success
- become more competent, confident and expert in their techniques.

Differentiation and Extension

Easier

- Set a shorter time.
- Incorporate swimming aids into the set activities.
- Devise a set circuit with choices of activity at set points.

Harder

- Increase the number of activities to complete.
- Increase the speed of performance.
- Set a number of times for a circuit to be completed within a time limit.

Extension

- Set competitive team challenges.
- Devise circuits for the class to attempt.
- Incorporate additional challenges (eg carrying objects/shooting into a goal).

Full Activity Description

See whether pupils can beat the time or distance for a personal survival challenge. Carry out a challenge lasting 6–10 minutes involving swimming, surface diving, floating, sculling, and getting into and out of the water. Explore ways of improving efficiency and safety.

›››

GYMNASTICS

STARTS AND FINISHES

Information Sheet

Sit

V-sit

Tuck

Tuck support

1 knee

2 knees

Straddle stand

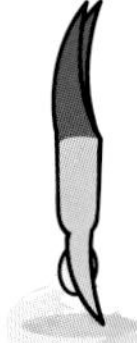
Handstand

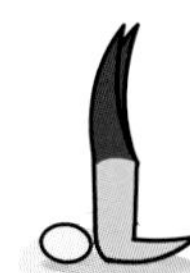
Shoulder balance

Prone support

TRAVEL

Information Sheet

Walk

Jog

Run

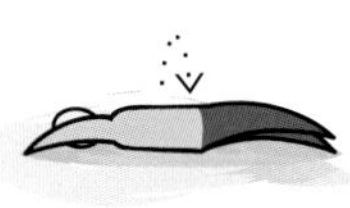

Roll

Hop

Skip

Sidestep

Crab

Bunny-hop

SHAPES

Information Sheet

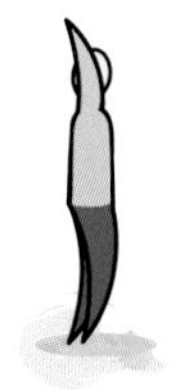
Straight

Arch

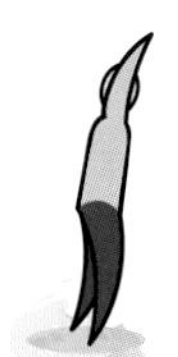
Chest pike

Pike

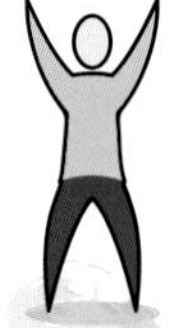
Straddle

Squat

Tuck

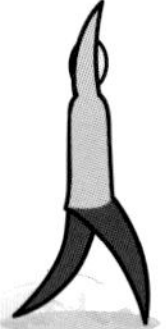
Lunge

Large

Small

ROLLS

Information Sheet

Log Tuck Teddy bear

Forward

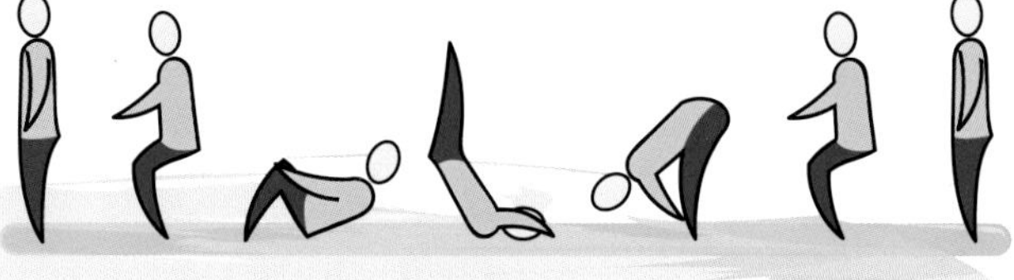

Backward

LINKS

Information Sheet

On

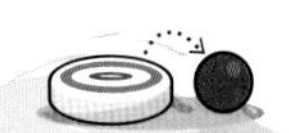
Off

Under

Over

High

Low

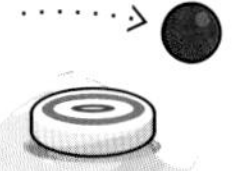
Across

Between

Fast

Slow

JUMPS

Information Sheet

Stretch

Tuck

Straddle

Pike

Split

Scissors

»» MAKE A SHORT MOVEMENT PHRASE

Activity 1, Pre-curriculum/Early Key Stage 1 (Age 4–5)

1 Choose **2** ways to **travel**.

2 Choose a **link** movement.

3 Choose a **shape** for the start and finish.

››› LEADER NOTES

Objectives

Pupils should:

- be able to perform a movement phrase in a given floor area
- know and understand what a 'movement phrase' is
- develop core movement, become increasingly competent and confident, and access a broad range of opportunities to extend their agility, balance and coordination, individually and with others.

Differentiation and Extension

Easier

- Use generic still shapes.
- Work in pairs/small groups.
- Copy/follow movements by a leader.

Harder

- Add more shapes.
- Define the travelling movements to be included.
- Add a time constraint/time for the movement phrase to last.

Extension

- Add levels, speeds, directions and pathways.
- Include movements of different body parts.
- Include movement on apparatus.

Full Activity Description

Choose 2 ways of travelling (eg walking backwards safely and a roll) and link these to make a short movement phrase you can remember and perform on the floor. Make sure you know where you start and finish, and what shapes you will make to start and finish.

LINK TOGETHER LIKE ACTIONS

Activity 2, Pre-curriculum/Early Key Stage 1 (Age 4–5)

1 Choose either **3**:

- **jumps**
- **rolls**
- ways of taking weight on your hands.

2 **Link** the movements together.

3 Repeat the movement phrase.

LEADER NOTES

Objectives

Pupils should:

- be able to identify and link like actions
- know and understand the term 'like actions'
- develop core movement, become increasingly competent and confident, and access a broad range of opportunities to extend their agility, balance and coordination, individually and with others.

Differentiation and Extension

Easier

- Use generic still shapes.
- Use low and single pieces of apparatus.
- Use fewer link actions.

Harder

- Link more actions in a sequence.
- Use higher apparatus.
- Use linked apparatus.

Extension

- Add levels, speeds, directions and pathways.
- Include movements of different body parts.

Full Activity Description

Choose 3 'like' actions (eg 3 different jumps, rolls or ways of taking your weight on your hands) and link these actions to make a short movement phrase on the floor and apparatus. You need to be able to remember and repeat your movement phrase.

››› MAKE A SEQUENCE USING ELEMENTS

Activity 3, Middle to Upper Key Stage 1 (Age 6–7)

1 Choose either **4**:

- **balances**
- **jumps**
- **rolls**
- **shapes.**

2 Choose a clear **start** position.

3 Move smoothly between shapes and actions.

»» LEADER NOTES

Objectives

Pupils should:

- be able to identify and link elements
- know and understand the term 'elements'
- develop core movement, become increasingly competent and confident, and access a broad range of opportunities to extend their agility, balance and coordination, individually and with others.

Differentiation and Extension

Easier

- Use generic still shapes.
- Work in pairs/small groups.
- Use fewer link actions.

Harder

- Link more actions in a sequence.
- Use contrasting actions.
- Repeat using different actions and directions.

Extension

- Add levels, speeds, directions and pathways.
- Include movements of different body parts.

Full Activity Description

Create and perform a simple sequence, on the floor and using mats, of up to 4 elements (eg balance, roll, jump and body shape). Make sure you have a clear starting position and move smoothly between shapes and actions.

PERFORM WITH A PARTNER

Activity 4, Middle to Upper Key Stage 1 (Age 6–7)

1 Choose apparatus to add to your sequence of **4** elements.

2 Add a partner's sequence to yours.

3 Perform the new sequence as a pair. Use apparatus, the floor and mats.

LEADER NOTES

Objectives

Pupils should:

- be able to combine 2 sequences
- know and understand how to link floor and apparatus movements together
- develop core movement, become increasingly competent and confident, and access a broad range of opportunities to extend their agility, balance and coordination, individually and with others.

Differentiation and Extension

Easier

- Use lower and separated apparatus.
- Use fewer link actions in the sequence.

Harder

- Vary the link movement between actions.
- Use higher, linked apparatus.

Extension

- Add levels, speeds, directions and pathways.
- Perform a sequence using different apparatus.

Full Activity Description

Transfer your sequence to a combination of floor, mats and apparatus (eg move from the floor to finish on apparatus, or move from apparatus to finish on the floor). Work with a partner to combine your sequence with theirs. Perform the new sequence as a pair.

PERFORM A SEQUENCE OF CONTRASTING ACTIONS

Activity 5, Upper Key Stage 1 (Age 6–7)

1 Link together contrasting actions:

- **– jumps**
- **– shapes**
- **– balances.**

2 Show **extension** in your balances.

3 Make your movements and actions flow together.

LEADER NOTES

Objectives

Pupils should:

- be able to perform a sequence that 'flows'
- know and understand the terms 'contrast' and 'extension'
- develop core movement, become increasingly competent and confident, and access a broad range of opportunities to extend their agility, balance and coordination, individually and with others.

Differentiation and Extension

Easier

- Make shorter sequences.
- Use fewer actions.

Harder

- Make longer sequences.
- Use more and complex actions.
- Repeat the sequence with a new emphasis.

Extension

- Add levels, speeds, directions and pathways.
- Perform sequences in small groups.
- Perform sequences using apparatus.

Full Activity Description

Using the floor and apparatus, create and perform a sequence of contrasting actions (eg 3 jumps and 2 balances), showing contrasting shapes. Make sure you show extension when balancing and flow when transferring your weight so the end of 1 action is the beginning of another.

PERFORM A SEQUENCE AT DIFFERENT SPEEDS

Activity 6, Upper Key Stage 1 (Age 6–7)

1 Choose 3 **balances**.

2 Link each balance with a different way of **travelling**.

3 Link the movements and actions, showing clear changes of speed.

LEADER NOTES

Objectives

Pupils should:

- be able to perform a sequence showing clear changes of speed
- know and understand different ways to balance
- develop core movement, become increasingly competent and confident, and access a broad range of opportunities to extend their agility, balance and coordination, individually and with others.

Differentiation and Extension

Easier

- Make shorter sequences.
- Use fewer actions.

Harder

- Make longer sequences.
- Use more and complex actions.
- Repeat the sequence with a new emphasis.

Extension

- Add levels, speeds, directions and pathways.
- Perform sequences in small groups.
- Perform sequences using apparatus.

Full Activity Description

Using the floor and mats, create and perform a sequence that involves a clear change of speed, linking 3 balances with 3 different ways of travelling (eg balance, travel, balance, travel, travel, balance).

››› PERFORM A SEQUENCE WITH 6 ELEMENTS

Activity 7, Upper Key Stage 1/Lower to Middle Key Stage 2 (Age 7–9)

1 Create a sequence with **6** elements
(eg twisting **shapes** or turning while **travelling**).

2 Teach your sequence to a partner.

3 Perform your sequence with your partner. Start and finish at the same time.

LEADER NOTES

Objectives

Pupils should:

- be able to perform a sequence in time with a partner
- know and understand how to teach a sequence to a partner
- develop core movement, become increasingly competent and confident, and access a broad range of opportunities to extend their agility, balance and coordination, individually and with others
- continue to implement and develop a broader range of skills, learning how to use them in different ways and link them to make actions and sequences of movement
- enjoy communicating and collaborating.

Differentiation and Extension

Easier

- Make shorter sequences.
- Use fewer elements.
- Copy a partner 1 element at a time.

Harder

- Make longer sequences.
- Include a change of dynamics (eg changes of level, speed or direction).
- Work in larger groups.

Extension

- Make another sequence using the same elements.
- Perform the same sequence incorporating apparatus.
- Join with another pair and swap partners during the sequence.

Full Activity Description

Create a sequence using the floor and mats that has up to 6 elements (eg 4 twisted shapes and 2 ways of turning while travelling). Teach your sequence to a partner, and then perform it so both of you start, perform and finish at the same time.

PERFORM WITH A PARTNER FROM START TO FINISH

Activity 8, Upper Key Stage 1/Lower to Middle Key Stage 2 (Age 7–9)

1 Create a sequence starting together with your partner.

2 Finish your sequence moving apart from your partner.

3 Include at least **4** elements following an L-shaped pathway.

Objectives

Pupils should:

- be able to perform a sequence following a pathway, in time with a partner
- know and understand how to sequence movements that move people together and apart
- develop core movement, become increasingly competent and confident, and access a broad range of opportunities to extend their agility, balance and coordination, individually and with others
- continue to implement and develop a broader range of skills, learning how to use them in different ways and link them to make actions and sequences of movement
- enjoy communicating and collaborating.

Differentiation and Extension

Easier

- Make shorter sequences.
- Use fewer elements.
- Copy a partner 1 element at a time.

Harder

- Make longer sequences.
- Include a change of dynamics (eg changes of level, speed or direction).
- Work in larger groups.

Extension

- Make another sequence using the same elements.
- Perform the same sequence incorporating apparatus.
- Join with another pair and swap partners during the sequence.

Full Activity Description

Using floor and apparatus, work with a partner to create and perform a sequence that involves both of you moving together from a starting point and then moving apart to finish. The sequence should include at least 4 elements, and each of you should follow an L-shaped pathway.

PERFORM A SEQUENCE WITH 8 ELEMENTS

Activity 9, Middle to Upper Key Stage 2 (Age 9–11)

1 Create a sequence with **8** elements. Include:

- asymmetrical **shapes** and **balances**
- symmetrical **rolls** and **jumping** actions.

2 Include changes of level and direction.

3 Include **mirroring** or **matching** shapes and balances.

>>> LEADER NOTES

Objectives

Pupils should:

- be able to link and perform 8 sequential elements
- know and understand the terms 'asymmetrical', 'symmetrical', 'mirroring' and 'matching'
- continue to implement and develop a broader range of skills, learning how to use them in different ways and link them to make actions and sequences of movement
- enjoy communicating and collaborating.

Differentiation and Extension

Easier

- Make shorter sequences.
- Use fewer elements.
- Copy a partner 1 element at a time.

Harder

- Make longer sequences.
- Include a change of dynamics (eg changes of level, speed or direction).
- Work in larger groups.

Extension

- Make another sequence using the same elements.
- Perform the same sequence incorporating apparatus/a combination of floor and apparatus.
- Perform in larger groups and in canon.

Full Activity Description

Working with a partner or in a small group, and using floor and mats, create and perform a gymnastic sequence of at least 8 elements (eg a combination of asymmetrical shapes and balances, with symmetrical rolling and jumping actions). Your sequence should include changes of direction and level, and incorporate mirroring or matching shapes and balances.

PERFORM YOUR 8-ELEMENT SEQUENCE ON APPARATUS

Activity 10, Middle to Upper Key Stage 2 (Age 9–11)

1 Choose apparatus to perform the 8-element sequence on.

2 Start the sequence on 1 **level** of the apparatus.

- Move to the floor.
- Finish on a different **level** of the apparatus.

3 Start and finish the sequence at the same time as the rest of the group.

LEADER NOTES

Objectives

Pupils should:

- be able to link a sequence to include elements at 3 different levels
- know and understand how to perform at different levels
- continue to implement and develop a broader range of skills, learning how to use them in different ways and link them to make actions and sequences of movement
- enjoy communicating and collaborating.

Differentiation and Extension

Easier

- Make shorter sequences.
- Use fewer elements.
- Copy a partner 1 element at a time.

Harder

- Make longer sequences.
- Include a change of dynamics (eg changes of speed or direction).
- Work in larger groups.

Extension

- Make another sequence using the same elements.
- Perform in larger groups and in canon.

Full Activity Description

Adapt the floor and mat sequence you created in Activity 9 so it can be performed on apparatus that includes 2 sections with different levels. Design the sequence so you start on 1 level of the apparatus, move to the floor, and finish on a different level of apparatus. The group must start and finish the sequence at the same time.

PERFORM A SEQUENCE WITH 10 ELEMENTS

Activity 11, Upper Key Stage 2 (Age 10–11)

1 Create a sequence with 10 elements. Include:

- twisting and turning
- **flight**
- changes of direction and speed
- contrasting **shapes** and **balances**.

2 Perform on the floor and apparatus.

3 Perform in front of an audience.

LEADER NOTES

Objectives

Pupils should:

- be able to link and perform 10 sequential elements
- know and understand the term 'flight'
- continue to implement and develop a broader range of skills, learning how to use them in different ways and link them to make actions and sequences of movement
- enjoy communicating and collaborating.

Differentiation and Extension

Easier

- Make shorter sequences.
- Use fewer elements.
- Copy a partner 1 element at a time.

Harder

- Make longer sequences.
- Include a change of dynamics (eg changes of level, speed or direction).
- Work in larger groups.

Extension

- Make another sequence using the same elements.
- Perform the same sequence using different apparatus.
- Perform in larger groups and in canon.

Full Activity Description

Using what you know about composing a sequence, create and perform a sequence on floor and apparatus for an audience. Your sequence should include at least 8–10 elements (eg start on the floor, move on to apparatus, finish on the floor). It must also include twisting and turning, flight, changes of direction and speed, and contrasting shapes and balances.

PERFORM YOUR 10-ELEMENT SEQUENCE IN A SMALL GROUP

Activity 12, Upper Key Stage 2 (Age 10–11)

1 Perform a 10-element sequence in a group of 3 or 4.

2 Perform on the floor and apparatus.

3 Each person should start and finish in a different place.

>>> LEADER NOTES

Objectives

Pupils should:

- be able to adapt an individual sequence to become a group sequence
- know and understand how people can be arranged in different ways in 1 sequence
- continue to implement and develop a broader range of skills, learning how to use them in different ways and link them to make actions and sequences of movement
- enjoy communicating and collaborating.

Differentiation and Extension

Easier

- Make shorter sequences.
- Use fewer elements.
- Copy a partner 1 element at a time.

Harder

- Make longer sequences.
- Include a change of dynamics (eg changes of level, speed or direction).
- Work in larger groups.

Extension

- Make another sequence using the same elements.
- Perform the same sequence using different apparatus.
- Perform in larger groups and in canon.

Full Activity Description

Adapt the sequence you created in Activity 11 so it can be performed in a small group of 3 or 4, using the floor and apparatus so each person starts and finishes in a different place.

>>> PERFORM A 1-MINUTE PAIRED SEQUENCE

Activity 13, Upper Key Stage 2/Lower to Middle Key Stage 3 (Age 10–13)

1 Perform a 1-minute sequence on the floor with a partner.

Include at least:

- 6 different actions
- 4 **balances** (1 upside-down).

2 Relate the actions and **balances** to each other.

3 Do not have any physical contact.

LEADER NOTES

Objectives

Pupils should:

- be able to perform a sequence with a partner for 1 minute
- know and understand how to relate actions between a pair in a sequence
- continue to implement and develop a broader range of skills, learning how to use them in different ways and link them to make actions and sequences of movement
- enjoy communicating and collaborating
- build on and embed the physical development and skills learnt in Key Stages 1 and 2, become more competent, confident and expert in their techniques, and apply them across different sports and activities
- understand what makes a performance effective and how to apply these principles to their own and others' work.

Differentiation and Extension

Easier

- Make shorter sequences.
- Use fewer elements.
- Use support or help.

Harder

- Make longer sequences.
- Include specific actions/agilities.
- Work in larger groups.

Extension

- Vary sequences by changing shapes/ways of travelling.
- Fit short phrases of action to music.

Full Activity Description

With a partner, create and perform a pair sequence on the floor lasting about 1 minute. Make sure you use skills and ideas from this unit. Your sequence must:

- include at least 6 different actions
- include at least 4 balances (some of which must be upside-down)
- show how you and your partner relate your own actions and balances to each other.

There must not be any physical contact between you and your partner.

JOIN 2 PAIRED SEQUENCES

Activity 14, Upper Key Stage 2/Lower to Middle Key Stage 3 (Age 10–13)

1 With another pair, combine 1-minute sequences to make a group sequence on the floor/using apparatus.

2 Plan for pathways:

– towards, away, parallel.

3 Plan for relationships:

– linked, using some physical support, separate, symmetrical, asymmetrical.

4 Plan for timing:

– matched, mirrored, canon, unison.

LEADER NOTES

Objectives

Pupils should:

- be able to create a sequence, planning for pathways, relationships and timing
- know and understand the terms 'parallel', 'linked', 'canon' and 'unison'
- continue to implement and develop a broader range of skills, learning how to use them in different ways and link them to make actions and sequences of movement
- enjoy communicating and collaborating
- build on and embed the physical development and skills learnt in Key Stages 1 and 2, become more competent, confident and expert in their techniques, and apply them across different sports and activities
- understand what makes a performance effective and how to apply these principles to their own and others' work.

Differentiation and Extension

Easier

- Make shorter sequences.
- Use fewer elements.
- Use support or help.

Harder

- Make longer sequences.
- Include specific actions/agilities.
- Work in larger groups.

Extension

- Vary sequences by changing shapes/ways of travelling.
- Fit short phrases of action to music.

Full Activity Description

Using the ideas and actions you used in your pairs sequence, join with another pair and combine the 2 sequences to produce a group sequence either on the floor or using apparatus. Make sure you plan for pathways (eg towards, away, parallel), relationships (eg linked, using some physical support, separate, symmetrical, asymmetrical) and timing (eg matched, mirrored, canon, unison).

PERFORM APPARATUS SEQUENCE

Activity 15, Upper Key Stage 2/Lower to Middle Key Stage 3 (Age 11–13)

1 In a group of 2 or 3, perform an apparatus sequence with 6–8 actions. Include:

- **flights**
- **rolls**
- **balances.**

2 Focus on carrying weight on the hands.

3 Perform **synchronised**, in canon or a mixture, with no physical contact.

LEADER NOTES

Objectives

Pupils should:

- be able to combine actions carrying weight on the hands into an apparatus sequence
- know and understand the term 'synchronised'
- continue to implement and develop a broader range of skills, learning how to use them in different ways and link them to make actions and sequences of movement
- enjoy communicating and collaborating
- build on and embed the physical development and skills learnt in Key Stages 1 and 2, become more competent, confident and expert in their techniques, and apply them across different sports and activities
- understand what makes a performance effective and how to apply these principles to their own and others' work.

Differentiation and Extension

Easier

- Make shorter sequences.
- Use fewer elements.
- Use support or help.

Harder

- Make longer sequences.
- Include specific actions.

Extension

- Perform sequences with different partners.
- Swap and perform partner's roles.

Full Activity Description

In groups of 2 or 3, pupils design and then perform an apparatus sequence of 6–8 actions incorporating flight, rolls and balances, which focus on carrying weight on hands. It must be synchronised or in canon, or be a mixture, and should involve no partner contact.

PERFORM SEQUENCE WITH PARTNER CONTACT SHAPES

Activity 16, Upper Key Stage 2/Lower to Middle Key Stage 3 (Age 11–13)

1 In a group of 2 or 3, perform a floor sequence.

2 Include 4–6 still **partner contact shapes.**

3 Link the sequence using actions. Include:

- rotation
- **flight**
- other forms of travelling.

LEADER NOTES

Objectives

Pupils should:

- be able to perform contact shapes that support part, and all, of a partner's weight
- know and understand the term 'partner contact shapes'
- continue to implement and develop a broader range of skills, learning how to use them in different ways and link them to make actions and sequences of movement
- enjoy communicating and collaborating
- build on and embed the physical development and skills learnt in Key Stages 1 and 2, become more competent, confident and expert in their techniques, and apply them across different sports and activities
- understand what makes a performance effective and how to apply these principles to their own and others' work.

Differentiation and Extension

Easier

- Give set actions to use.
- Use fewer actions/shorter sequences.
- Use support or help.

Harder

- Make longer sequences.
- Include more/specific actions.
- Introduce time constraints/speed.

Extension

- Perform sequences with different partners.
- Swap and perform partner's roles (safety and weight permitting).

Full Activity Description

In groups of 2 or 3, pupils create and then perform a sequence on the floor, incorporating 4–6 still partner contact shapes. Contacts can include supporting part or all of a partner's weight. Link the sequence using actions involving rotation, flight and other forms of travelling.

››› DANCE

MAKE YOUR OWN DANCE

Activity 1, Pre-curriculum/Early Key Stage 1 (Age 5–6)

1 Choose a theme for your dance.

2 Choose shapes and actions to suit your theme.

3 Choose a start and finish for your dance.

LEADER NOTES

Objectives

Pupils should:

- be able to link and perform a series of movements based on an imaginary character
- know and understand the term 'theme' when used in the dance and movement context
- develop fundamental movement skills, become increasingly competent and confident, and access a broad range of opportunities to extend their agility, balance and coordination.

Differentiation and Extension

Easier

- Use an adult and/or pairs to dance together.
- Copy the movements of a character (eg a clown/penguin) or the dancing actions of a confident person.
- Create small repeated and similar phrases.

Harder

- Include rhythms and changes of speed.
- Use large spaces with levels and directions.
- Make the dance last for a set period of time.

Extension

- Explore making different shapes.
- Explore TV programme or book characters.
- Perform dances to pop songs.

Full Activity Description

Create, perform and share short dances based on themes such as:

- clowns – funny walking patterns, balancing, tumbling, jumping, falling
- penguins – huddling, flapping, waddling
- folk dance patterns – dancing in a circle, skipping to the centre and out, clapping and stamping a pattern on the spot, walking backwards and forwards in a chain.

Make sure you can remember how to start and finish your dance, and what shapes or actions you have in the middle. Make sure these are always the same.

MAKE A DANCE TO SHOW DIFFERENT MOODS

Activity 2, Middle to Upper Key Stage 1 (Age 6–7)

1 Act out different **moods**:

– happy, sad, angry.

2 Make a dance to show the **moods**.

3 Make your dance energetic and emotional.

LEADER NOTES

Objectives

Pupils should:

- be able to guess the mood an individual is dancing
- know and understand the terms 'energetic' and 'emotional' when used in the dance and movement context
- develop fundamental movement skills, become increasingly competent and confident, and access a broad range of opportunities to extend their agility, balance and coordination
- be able to engage in a range of increasingly challenging situations.

Differentiation and Extension

Easier

- Use an adult and/or pairs to dance together.
- Play 'guess the mood' games in pairs before adding dance actions.
- Create small repeated and similar phrases.

Harder

- Include rhythms and changes of speed.
- Use large spaces with levels and directions.
- Incorporate less obvious emotions, such as 'confused' or 'worried'.

Extension

- Explore comparisons to moods (eg the sea, weather, seasons).
- Explore the movements of a changing situation (eg a growing flower, a raging bull).

Full Activity Description

Create and perform short dances using rhythm and expressive and dynamic qualities to show different moods, ideas and feelings. You could use stimuli such as **Ananse and the Sky God** with:

- sad children – walking and stopping, droopy, slow, slumped shapes
- angry sky god – angry, stamping, giant-like steps; strong, sudden movements
- spider's web and climbing – weaving, zigzag curving, travelling patterns, climbing actions on the spot
- happy motif – skipping, hopping, running, shaking.

MAKE A DANCE THAT LOOKS LIKE MACHINERY

Activity 3, Upper Key Stage 1 (Age 6–7)

1 Show the cogs and machine parts working.

2 Show the machine parts working together.

3 Show the machine breaking down.

LEADER NOTES

Objectives

Pupils should:

- be able to guess which part of the machine 'cycle' an individual is dancing
- know and understand how to change speeds, strengths, levels and directions to look like a specific process
- develop fundamental movement skills, become increasingly competent and confident, and access a broad range of opportunities to extend their agility, balance and coordination
- be able to engage in a range of increasingly challenging situations on their own and with others.

Differentiation and Extension

Easier

- Use an adult and/or pairs to dance together.
- Play 'guess the action' games in pairs before adding dance actions.
- Create small repeated and similar phrases.

Harder

- Include rhythms and changes of speed.
- Use large spaces with levels and directions.
- Make longer dance phrases.

Extension

- Explore incorporating small parts (people) to make 1 large machine (group dance).
- Explore acting out/dancing other processes (eg getting into a car, starting it up and driving on different roads).

Full Activity Description

Create and perform a dance, on your own, with a partner or in a small group, on the idea of 'machines'. Make sure you use changes in speed, strength, level, direction and space in your dance. Include the following 3 sections in your dance:

- section 1 – cogs and pistons: circling; jerky; pulling; pushing; shaking; large; small; whole-body actions; individual body parts; quick and sudden; slow and controlled; speeding up; slowing down; on the spot; travelling; on your own; with a partner
- section 2 – working together: copying and following each other; moving in opposite directions; side by side; facing each other; moving in unison; in canon; meeting and parting; going over, under and round a partner
- section 3 –breakdown: out of control; spinning; jumping; racing; slowing and stopping.

MAKE A DANCE WITH CHARACTERS, MIRRORS, FIGHTS!

Activity 4, Upper Key Stage 1/Lower to Middle Key Stage 2 (Age 7–9)

1 Show lots of different people's personalities.

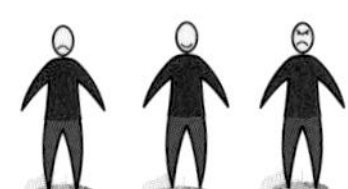

2 Show expressions after looking in mirrors.

3 Show fighting actions.

LEADER NOTES

Objectives

Pupils should:

- be able to act and dance in their character role
- know and understand how to maximise personalities by making powerful face and body movement changes
- become increasingly competent and confident, and access a broad range of opportunities to extend their agility, balance and coordination
- continue to apply and develop a broader range of skills, learning how to use them in different ways and link them to make actions and sequences of movement
- enjoy communicating and collaborating with each other
- learn how to evaluate and recognise their own success.

Differentiation and Extension

Easier

- Use an adult and/or pairs to dance together.
- Play guessing games in pairs before linking dance movements.
- Create small repeated and similar phrases.

Harder

- Include rhythms and changes of speed.
- Use large spaces with levels and directions.
- Make longer dance phrases.

Extension

- Explore acting out/dancing a TV advert.
- Explore acting out/dancing a short version of a play or film (eg Mr and Mrs Smith; The Stepford Wives [robots])

Full Activity Description

Create and perform dances based on characters and narrative, using the dance idea 'Welcome to the House of Fun'. The dance should have 2 or 3 sections, which could be based on:

- individual characters – body shape, travelling at different speeds, shy, giggling, kicking, punching
- hall of mirrors – developing body shapes using different levels; balancing; supporting; changing the group shape by moving under, round and through each other to create different still images (eg long, thin, contorted, wide, round, while pulling funny faces)
- a comic fight – (eg Popeye against Bluto) including action and reaction, and question and answer sequencing (eg swipe, turn, travel, swing, fall, lift, tumble, roll).

COPY AND PERFORM A FAMOUS DANCE

Activity 5, Middle to Upper Key Stage 2 (Age 9–11)

1 Watch the steps of a **famous** dance.

2 Learn the steps in a group.

3 Dance with your group in front of other people.

LEADER NOTES

Objectives

Pupils should:

- be able to copy and perform a famous dance routine
- know and understand the name of a famous dance and a series of patterns and steps within the dance
- continue to apply and develop a broader range of skills, learning how to use them in different ways and link them to make actions and sequences of movement
- enjoy communicating and collaborating with each other
- develop an understanding of how to improve, and learn how to evaluate and recognise their own success.

Differentiation and Extension

Easier

- Copy steps from a leader.
- Perform with partners.

Harder

- Perform in large groups or as a class.
- Interlink a series of patterns/sections.

Extension

- Lead 1 dance into another.
- Perform a 'dance-off' competition.

Full Activity Description

In groups, learn the patterns and structure for a set dance (eg the pavane) and then perform it to others.

MAKE AND PERFORM A DANCE WITH 3 SECTIONS

Activity 6, Middle to Upper Key Stage 2 (Age 9–11)

1 Make a dance with a **beginning, middle** and **end**.

2 Include **patterns** in your dance.

3 Include leaders and characters.

LEADER NOTES

Objectives

Pupils should:

- be able to remember and perform a made-up dance
- know and understand what constitutes a dance 'pattern' and the term 'dance phrase'
- continue to apply and develop a broader range of skills, learning how to use them in different ways and link them to make actions and sequences of movement
- enjoy communicating and collaborating with each other
- develop an understanding of how to improve, and learn how to evaluate and recognise their own success.

Differentiation and Extension

Easier

- Assign characters/patterns that must be included.
- Set short dance phrases.
- Use small amounts of space.

Harder

- Incorporate changes of rhythm and/or speed.
- Use larger spaces and include height and direction.
- Work in larger groups.

Extension

- Perform the partner's dance role.
- Nominate choreographers for sections and/or whole dances.

Full Activity Description

As a class, create and perform a dance with 3 sections. This might include:

- Tudor dance – a set dance focusing on performance style, patterning and timing
- patterns – using fabric and garden designs to create small group dances that develop step patterns, gestures and pathways
- the masque ball – a processional section with different leaders and characters (eg courtiers and jesters), which develops into a whole-class dance combining different formations, rhythms and patterns.

Working with your teacher, decide how individuals and groups will take on roles and sections of the dance. Try taking on your partner's role in the dance. Try being the choreographer for a small section of the dance.

MAKE A DANCE WITH IDEAS FROM A VIDEO

Activity 7, Upper Key Stage 2 (Age 10–11)

1 Make a dance with your own movements, **style**,

structure and **patterns**.

2 Get ideas from watching a silent video.

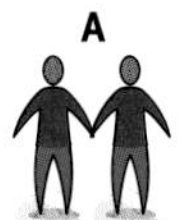

3 Repeat sections in a **pattern** (eg A, B, A, B, C).

LEADER NOTES

Objectives

Pupils should:

- be able to use a visual film to inspire dance movements
- know and understand the dance terms 'meeting', 'parting', 'unison' and 'anon'
- continue to apply and develop a broader range of skills, learning how to use them in different ways and link them to make actions and sequences of movement
- enjoy communicating and collaborating with each other
- develop an understanding of how to improve, and learn how to evaluate and recognise their own success.

Differentiation and Extension

Easier

- Assign characters/patterns that must be included.
- Set short dance phrases.
- Use small amounts of space.

Harder

- Incorporate changes of rhythm and/or speed.
- Use larger spaces and include height and direction.
- Work in larger groups.

Extension

- Perform the partner's dance role.
- Nominate choreographers for sections and/or whole dances.

Full Activity Description

In pairs or small groups, create and perform a dance. Use a short video extract (eg 'Humboldt's Hog Nose Flea Dance' from 'Still Life at the Penguin Café', 'Cats' [Andrew Lloyd Webber] or 'West Side Story') to inspire your movements and ideas. For example, you could base your dance on an idea such as 'comical folk', human animals or fitting in with a gang.

Take ideas from the video, choosing:

- movements and actions (eg skipping, hopping, jumping, lifting, supporting, different body shapes, stamping and striking sticks)
- dance style
- structure (eg solo, partner and group work; meeting, parting, over, under, around, follow, unison, canon)
- patterning (eg circling, weaving, straight lines, facing).

Make sure you plan a dance framework for 1, 2, 3 or 4 sections, with different forms such as AB, ABA, ABCDAB. You need to choose which sections individuals dance, and which in pairs or groups. Try taking on someone else's role in the dance. Try being the choreographer, or costume or set designer.

»» MAKE SHORT 'STEP AND ACTION' DANCES

Activity 8, Upper Key Stage 2/Key Stage 3 (Age 10–14)

1 Make a short dance from **3** famous dances.

2 Add short dances together to make a long dance.

3 Join with a partner/group to perform.